THE
NILE
AND ITS PEOPLE

THE
NILE
AND ITS PEOPLE

7000 YEARS OF EGYPTIAN HISTORY

CHARLOTTE BOOTH

The
History
Press

First published 2010

The History Press
The Mill, Brimscombe Port
Stroud, Gloucestershire, GL5 2QG
www.thehistorypress.co.uk

British Library Cataloguing in Publication Data.
A catalogue record for this book is available from the British Library.

ISBN 978 0 7524 5506 8

Typesetting and origination by The History Press
Printed in Great Britain
Manufacturing managed by Jellyfish Print Solutions Ltd

CONTENTS

ACKNOWLEDGEMENTS

I have had a great deal of support whilst writing this book and would like to thank everyone who has given me encouragement, kind words and much-needed glasses of wine. In particular I would like to thank the Thomas Cook Archive, the Griffith Institute, Sonia Brasseur, Peter Billington and Brian Billington.

ILLUSTRATIONS

All photographs and drawings by the author unless otherwise stated.

COLOUR PLATES

1   Sunset over the Nile at Luxor
2   The Holy Family in Egypt. Hanging Church, Cairo
3   Scorpion Macehead. Ashmoleon Museum. (Courtesy of Brian Billington)
4   Pleasure Lake from the tomb of Nebamun (eighteenth dynasty). British Museum
5   Sacred lake at Medinet Habu
6   The golden mask of Psusennes from Tanis. The Ancient Egypt Picture Library
7   The silver anthropoid coffin of Psusennes from Tanis. The Ancient Egypt Picture Library
8   Greek graffiti on the leg of the southern colossi of Memnon
9   Alexander the Great. (Courtesy of Photos.com)
10   Ibn Tulun Mosque, Cairo. (Courtesy of Brian Billington)
11   Islamic Cairo at night.
12   Battle of the Pyramids. (Courtesy of Photos.com)
13   Champollion defaces a pillar with his name at Karnak
14   Thomas Cook tour poster. (Courtesy of the Thomas Cook Archives)
15   Temple of Debod, Madrid. (Courtesy of Photos.com)

MONO FIGURES

1   Reconstructed boat of Khufu at Giza
2   Swimming girl cosmetic spoon. Ashmoleon Museum, Oxford. (Courtesy of Brian Billington)

MAPS

INTRODUCTION

On a hot dry day in June 1881 the Nile saw the last 'funeral' of ancient pharaohs in Egypt. The final journey of 40 royal mummies began on the west
bank, near Deir el Bahri at Luxor, where they were loaded onto barges to be
shipped to their final resting place at the Egyptian Museum in Cairo. Some of
the most famous kings in Egyptian history were part of this funeral, including
Ahmose, Amenhotep I, Tuthmosis III, Sety I, Ramses II and Ramses III. Their
final journey along the Nile, a river that would be a familiar sight to all of them,
was one of reverence and sadness, even 3500 years after their deaths and original entombment. Although not accompanied by treasures of gold, a large crowd
gathered to pay their respects. Throughout the long trip the banks of the Nile
were lined with mourners: women clad from head to toe in black, making eerie
wails, as they flagellated themselves, tearing at their hair in a public demonstration
of grief. These women were accompanied by men displaying their grief by shooting rifles in the air. Although the world these Egyptians lived in was very different
to that of their ancestors they felt the need to mourn, paying respect to the long
dead. It would have made a truly remarkable sight.

So what led to the Nile being used for this mournful procession? The 40
mummies formed the royal cache discovered in 1871 in a tomb at Deir el Bahri
by the Rassoul brothers who lived at Gourna. The brothers were well known
to the Egyptian authorities as robbers, making a living by pillaging tombs and
selling their bounty to wealthy tourists. One of the brothers discovered the
tomb accidentally and slowly the family started to leak the artefacts onto the
market, carefully keeping the source a secret. As more relics appeared it captured
the attention of the authorities and Gaston Maspero, the Director General of
Antiquities, ordered their arrest and interrogation. The brothers would not reveal

the secret of their source, so Maspero sent Ahmed Basha Kamal to speak to two other siblings, Ahmed and Hussein. Despite various methods of interrogation, they still refused to give up the secret. However, once they were released a family squabble ensued, as Hussein and Ahmed demanded a higher share of the profits due to the torture they had endured. This squabble escalated until Mohamed, another brother, went to the local authorities, revealing the location of the tomb. The authorities telegrammed Emille Brugsch, Maspero's assistant in Cairo, who travelled to Luxor before being taken to the tomb on 6 June 1881; a full 10 years after the brothers initially found it. Brugsch was lowered into the tomb by a rope and was amazed at what he saw:

> Soon we came upon cases of porcelain funeral offerings, metal and alabaster vessels, draperies and trinkets, until, reaching the turn in the passage, a cluster of mummy cases came to view in such number as to stagger me ... Collecting my senses, I made the best examination of them I could by the light of my torch and at once saw that they contained the mummies of royal personages of both sexes; and yet that was not all. Plunging on ahead ... I came to see the chamber and there, standing against the walls or lying on the floor, I found an even greater number of mummy cases of stupendous size and weight. Their gold coverings and their polished surfaces so plainly reflected my own excited visage that it seemed as though I was looking into the faces of my own ancestors.[1]

This collection of mummies had been moved from the Valley of the Kings and rewrapped in the twenty-first dynasty (1069–945 BCE) by the Priests of Amun to protect them from tomb robbery. They were successful in this for nearly 3000 years, until the Rassoul brothers discovered their hiding place. In just 10 days the authorities cleared the tomb and the 40 mummies were loaded onto a paddle steamer to be taken to Cairo, where they remain today. The identities of 32 of the mummies have since been discovered and work continues today on the remaining eight.

Although a fabulous story of tomb robbers and treasure, one of the most intriguing aspects of the event was the use of the Nile to transport the mummies to their final destination. This emphasises the importance of the Nile both in 1881 CE, when it was the quickest form of transportation between Luxor and Cairo in anticipation of the railway built in 1898, and in ancient times when it was an important element of ancient Egyptian royal funerals. This Nile procession continued a tradition thousands of years old as a means for the king or the god to be visible to the people along the banks.

From the earliest times the Nile was used to transport both the living and the dead, including the deceased king. The only reconstructed funeral boat, that of

Khufu (2589–2566 BCE) at Giza, is generally accepted to be the vessel that transported his mummy from the royal residence on the east bank to the mortuary temple on the west bank before being transferred to the pyramid (fig. 1). The journey from the river to the Great Pyramid was shorter then than now due to a migration of the Nile which will be discussed in the following chapters. The procession from the east to the west bank represented the king's passing from the land of the living (east) to that of the dead (west), and although royal funerals were not recorded, the combination of the cedar funerary boat of Khufu, images of Nile processions and reliefs of non-royal funerals help produce a plausible scenario of the splendour of such a funeral. It would have been a solemn journey with the silence broken only by 10 oars hitting the water and the wailing of the professional mourners hired for the occasion. Behind the royal barge would have been numerous smaller vessels bearing funerary goods to be used by the king in the afterlife which would be carried in procession to the tomb. Although in 1881 funerary goods were not part of the procession, the number of mummies meant that more than one vessel was needed, perhaps presenting a very similar scene to those of ancient times. These 5000 years of continuity are not accidental but rather an expected result of the Egyptians' reliance on the river, suggesting certain aspects of culture will remain for as long as this dependency exists.

The Nile is the longest river in the world, flowing from East Africa to the Mediterranean, a total distance of 6741km with only 1553km in Egypt and the vast majority in Sudan. Despite this, the river Nile is commonly associated with Egypt. The question arises as to why this should be the case and why I have written a new book focusing specifically on the civilisation of the Egyptian stretch of the Nile rather than the Sudanese.

One of the main reasons for this focus is knowledge. There is so much available information about the ancient Egyptian civilisation alongside the Nile from archaeological evidence and written documentation that it is possible to create a virtually unbroken historical record from 30,000 BCE to the modern day. The written record is key, however, in the reconstruction as the earliest written record dates to 3100 BCE, whereas the earliest identified Nubian text identified dates to the eighth century CE. Although the Egyptian script was used in Egyptian ruled Nubia, the lack of an indigenous written language means there are many gaps in the history of the region. The archaeological record can only be interpreted to a certain extent but can never clearly identify events and beliefs. Therefore, the record from Egypt enables me to present a complete yet condensed history and this is what follows.

The Nile was the source of everything in ancient Egypt; the source of all life and sometimes of death. This duality of life and death is a fundamental characteristic of the Nile that the people living under its influence were and still are acquainted with. Dual nature became an aspect of all religion and life; life and death (the Nile); dark and light (the sun); east and west (the land); Upper and Lower Egypt (political division); and chaos and order (kingship). The foundations of the Egyptian belief system were that without one thing the other could not exist and this also applied to the Nile; with the good (life and sustenance) came the bad (death and destruction), leading people to have respect for this mighty river, not to take it for granted and, to a certain extent, fear it. This fear of the destructive side of the Nile is not, however, an ancient phenomenon, hindered by lack of technology. Four serious floods between 1860 and 1880 resulted in a number of deaths even with thousands of years' experience in dealing with it. With the construction of the High Dam in 1971 one of the main concerns with the design was the destruction that would befall Egypt should the dam ever be bombed. This was never solved and, should this ever happen, Egypt as we know it would no longer exist. Even with modern technology the Nile can only be tamed to a certain degree, meaning the fear of death and destruction is always present.

1 Reconstructed boat of Khufu at Giza

Despite the danger, the Nile has been manipulated throughout its history for food, transport and pleasure, and life has been greatly enhanced for the Egyptians (both ancient and modern) by this body of water. Because the nature of the Nile has not changed in thousands of years, neither has its usage and the modern traveller to Egypt, especially in the rural areas, will still see women washing their clothes and cooking utensils in the water, farmers watering their animals and children swimming and playing in the shallows – exactly the same as 4000 years ago. The people have changed in that time, but the Nile has not. It has remained a constant element, shaping the lives of those who live alongside it.

This continuity of culture and Nile manipulation is the focus of this book, differing in many ways from other books of Egyptian history. Because the Nile is so fundamental to the lives of the Egyptians, both ancient and modern, it is essential to look at their history and the river in conjunction with each other. It would be impossible to look at them in isolation, as without the Nile, Egypt and her civilisation could not exist, and yet without the civilisation the Nile would not be as significant as it is. It is something that is synonymous with Egypt and is considered an identifying characteristic of the country. It is almost a mythical being, with one author comparing its journey from the source to the Mediterranean with the passing of a human lifetime, sharing characteristics with youth, adolescence, adulthood and old age. Various texts, films and artwork emphasise the romanticism and exoticism of the waters, until it became more than just a waterway but rather a thing of legend. The mythologising of the Nile and its characteristics need to be investigated to truly understand the importance of the river to the people, both spiritually and practically.

Through the following chapters we will investigate the changing community, culture and practices of the Egyptian people, from the hunter-gatherer tribes to those of modern times, and the relationship they each share with the Nile. We will investigate the ways in which the river has been manipulated for pleasure, agriculture and tourism, as well as the role it played in the rediscovery of the Egyptian civilisation. One thing that will become clear is that the Nile was and is bigger than the population and culture surrounding it.

The ancient Egyptians appreciated the importance of this river and knew it both gave and took life, and could never truly be under the control of mankind. For this reason they personified the Nile in the form of Hapy, the god of the Nile inundation, and through the worship of Hapy they hoped to control the waters, suppressing its destructive side. Sometimes they were successful but only at the behest of the god. In the following pages we will see the history of Egypt through the eyes of Hapy, the Nile god, witnessing the civilisation of Egypt and the control the river had over it.

𓃻 1 𓃻

WE NEED NOT SLEEP TO DREAM

THE MYTH OF THE NILE

The Nile was essential to the survival of the ancient Egyptians, who relied on it for water, transportation and the fertile silt deposited over the fields after the annual inundation. This was the case until the High Dam at Aswan was opened in 1971, curbing the inundation and providing a much more stable environment for Egypt. Although modern Egyptians do not rely on the silt deposited by the inundation, without the Nile their fields would not be irrigated and their crops would not grow; now, as in the past, the Egyptians are totally dependent on the river.

Although this dependency is a localised phenomenon affecting only the countries through which the Nile flows, the river is as much a part of Western culture as it is of Egyptian. For the Egyptians the Nile was and is their life-force – as essential to life as breathing – whereas for Westerners it is viewed as a playground – an exotic waterway emanating wealth, luxury and decadence.

The same associations of wealth and luxury are not afforded to the Ganges in India, the waters of Venice or the Thames in London, although they certainly have their own myths. So why is the Nile seen in this way? Is it a modern construct or has this process been in motion for centuries with each generation building on the myths of the past? Evidence would suggest this myth of the Nile as something other than a river has in fact been developing since the time of the pharaohs, and continues evolving even to the modern day. In order to unravel this myth, it is essential to identify what it is and what it means in the modern Western world.

The Nile is invariably associated with Egypt rather than the Sudan, and in particular luxury cruises (plate 1), seen as the ultimate in holiday decadence. It was described by Jules Verne Travel Company as a 'rare opportunity to enjoy the natural beauty of the river and the ancient civilisation of Egypt in an atmosphere of period elegance – almost in the style of a "house party" from earlier times'; these cruises of 'earlier times' being those of the nineteenth and twentieth centuries when groups of wealthy tourists would board a paddle steamer and cruise the Nile from Alexandria to Aswan. This type of cruise was immortalised in Agatha Christie's *Death on the Nile* as a number of the 'fashionable elite' set sail from Aswan on such a boat accompanied by Hercule Poirot. In the television productions of *Death on the Nile* the scenery is integral to the exotic and awe-inspiring atmosphere and has made both the book and dramatisation popular. The novel itself is somewhat lacking in description of the Nile or the surrounding scenery and there are only two descriptions: one of the rocks at the first cataract at Aswan and the other of the main temple at Abu Simbel, although Christie does not mention its name until the following chapter. It is assumed that the reader is familiar with the scenery and monuments, rendering it unnecessary to name them. In fact, one could go as far to say that in regard to the plot of *Death on the Nile*, there was no need for the story to take place in Egypt at all except for two points. The main characters needed to be wealthy and it was essential they were unable to leave the premises. So to accommodate both of these, the Nile cruise was chosen, conveying a message to the readers of luxury, decadence and wealth without needing to vocalise it. Therefore, although this novel is often stated as the source of the Nile cruise obsession with Western travellers, it is clear in 1937 the association of it with luxury and wealth already existed. The earliest evidence of this association dates from the middle fifteenth century CE with the introduction of the printing press. Numerous travel books about Egypt were translated into various languages, encouraging the wealthy to embark on a voyage. Much of the information published was inaccurate or the stuff of myths, but it led to an interest in Egypt which has continued to develop.

The eighteenth and nineteenth centuries saw an increase in travellers to Egypt, and at the height of the Grand Tour there was an increase in antiquarianism and archaeological interest in all things Egyptian. This led to great rivalry between collectors of ancient artefacts, resulting in illicit digging of tombs in the hunt for relics to sell to tourists. This increased once the hieroglyphic language was deciphered in 1822. Before the decipherment it was simply fashionable to have Egyptian artefacts, but after it caused a frenetic *need* for inscriptions to help unravel the ancient secrets.

From the 1840s onwards, rather than hiring a paddle steamer to traverse the Nile, most wealthy individuals hired a *dahibeya* (a flat-bottomed wooden houseboat). However, many travellers from Alexandria were more concerned with travelling southwards as quickly as possible than viewing the ancient ruins; and these journeys rarely included excursions to the monuments. Instead they were viewed from the boat.[1] Amelia Edwards commented on the folly of this, as at the time the banks of the Nile were higher than the eye line of the people on the boat, severely limiting what they could see. The journey northwards with the current was, however, taken at a more leisurely pace with more opportunities to stop and sightsee.

In the 1860s Thomas Cook and Sons introduced the 'package tour' to Egypt with steam boats, holding more passengers and travelling faster than the *dahibeya*. It would therefore seem that whilst tourism was older, cruising down the Nile on a hired boat as the height of rich decadent living originated in the nineteenth century. The earliest evidence we have, however, of a Nile cruise was carried out by Cleopatra VII in 47 CE. She was 23 years old and pregnant with Julius Caesar's child. They sailed down the Nile from Alexandria, stopping at the Pyramids and Denderah before reaching Thebes to visit the temple at Karnak. Although used as a political tool, it was clearly a pleasure cruise stopping at well-known sites along the way.

The Nile cruises today are nothing compared to the experience of Cleopatra. Most cruises now are only in the south, as the number of bridges in the north makes it impossible for the boats to pass. The course of the Nile has also altered since the time of Cleopatra, and mooring at the pyramids of Giza is no longer possible. Modern Nile cruises also do not compare to those of the nineteenth and early twentieth century and are no longer the sojourn of the rich and famous. A week-long cruise is no longer a holiday of a lifetime; an all-inclusive trip will cost a few hundred pounds – cheaper than a week in a European city. Although cruises are a fantastic way of covering a large portion of Upper Egypt, they are far from the relaxing tours of the 1920s and 1930s, with many tours starting at 5.30 a.m. However, they are still marketed as the luxury of days gone by with an 'atmosphere of period elegance'.[2]

Visitors feel they are walking in the footsteps of famous, historical figures, upon what has been explained as the 'world's most history-laden waterway'.[3] What adds more romance to a cruise or a holiday than the knowledge that Julius Caesar and Cleopatra did it before you? Or that one is walking in the footsteps of Ramses II? Or even that one is following the trail of the Christian holy family whilst in the streets of Cairo? The answer is very little, and this is something modern holiday companies have embraced: the themed tour. A common theme being the Ramses II tour, as this enigmatic nineteenth-dynasty king left his mark in most areas of Egypt from the Delta to Nubia – making for a diverse and interesting itinerary. Other popular trips are Biblical tours; either following the route of the Exodus or the journey of the holy family in Egypt. Both of these feature the Nile as an important element.

Although the story of the Exodus has no supporting archaeological evidence[4] and there is no clear indication of when the Exodus occurred or any proof of the existence of Moses, it is a very important text describing how Moses freed thousands of slaves from Egyptian oppression, leading them to the Promised Land, which is now the nation of Israel. Regardless of whether it is historical fact or not, its importance cannot be denied. The beginning of the Exodus story involves the birth of Moses, born after an unnamed Egyptian king decreed all male Hebrew children were to be drowned in the Nile. In order to save Moses, his mother Jochebed placed him within a basket and set him adrift on the Nile. Miriam, his sister, watched as the basket drifted to an area where the king's daughter was swimming with her servants (fig. 2). The princess spotted the basket and demanded it be brought to her. As the princess had no children she was unable to nurse the child, so Miriam approached her and asked whether she would accept a Hebrew nurse. Jochebed therefore nursed Moses, who was raised as the child of the princess.

The nature of the Nile in this narrative is two-fold: both the cause of life and death. The king planned to kill the boys in the Nile and Moses was offered a new life, almost a rebirth, from the very same waters. This duality of the nature of the Nile is a very Egyptian idea, and a fundamental part of the story. The creative elements of the Nile are also represented, as a child was produced from the waters for the childless princess; something else that appealed to the Egyptian mindset. The Nile in this story is the bringer of life, bringing a child to the childless and enabling Jochebed to save her son and offer him a new life in the palace.

This narrative is an important part of Western culture, and the name 'Moses basket' derived from this tale, and has ensconced the Nile in the mind as a sacred place, a place of great significance and importance. One could argue that without the Nile the Exodus could not have occurred at all, and eventual creation of the nation of Israel would not have happened.

Later in Biblical history the Nile features in the story of the sojourn of the holy family into Egypt (plate 2) to escape death at the hands of King Herod. They were in Egypt for four years although only the start of the journey is recorded in the Bible:

> And when they [the wise men from the east] were departed, behold the angel of the Lord appeared to Joseph in a dream, saying, 'Arise, and take the young child and his mother, and flee into Egypt, and be thou there until I bring you word; for Herod will seek the young Child to destroy Him'. When he arose, he took the young Child and His mother by night and departed into Egypt; and was there until the death of Herod, that it might be fulfilled which was spoken of the Lord by the prophet, saying, 'Out of Egypt I called My Son'. (Matt. 2:13–15)

The journey of the holy family in Egypt has survived to the modern day in a mixture of Coptic texts from Egypt and Armenia. They started their journey by travelling by donkey across the Sinai, entering Egypt at the town of Pelusium on the Pelusaic branch of the Nile. They travelled through the Delta, by donkey initially, but records at the Church of the Blessed Virgin at Maadi in Cairo indicate that this was the point upon which they hired a boat and started their journey southwards on the Nile. The journey south was peppered by stops at various sites, each marked by a church or monument commemorating miracles or resting points. The site of Deir el Muharraq is particularly important as they stayed here

2 Swimming girl cosmetic spoon.
Ashmoleon Museum, Oxford
(*Courtesy of Brian Billington*)

for six months and five days. Their journey south, however, was to end at Deir Durunka, south of Assyut, where they resided in a cave before waiting for a boat to take them northwards so they could return to Palestine.

On the journey back to Palestine they stayed at Babylon (Cairo) in a cave. The Church of Saint Sergius (Abu Sargah) (fig. 3) now stands over the spot and has been a site of pilgrimage for hundreds of years. This subterranean cave flooded with the inundation and was under water for two months a year. The water which flowed into this 'sacred area' was considered holy. Whilst residing at Babylon, they visited the area of the Nile where the basket of Moses was drawn out by the Egyptian princess, the exact location being known at that time. It was thought the basket of Moses was stored in the Mosque of Tubah at Giza,[5] indicating this was near the sacred area. Whilst they were at Giza they saw the pyramids and although they had their minds on higher things it is an interesting consideration that they too gazed in awe at these great monuments.

When one considers the eminent people that have travelled on the Nile, including Tutankhamun, Ramses II, Julius Caesar, Cleopatra, Moses, Jesus and the Virgin Mary, moving on to Saladin, Napoleon, Mark Twain, Agatha Christie and William Golding and every well-known Egyptologist for the past 200 years, it is hardly surprising that the Nile has developed in the Western mind as a thing to be revered and held in awe. References to Egypt and the Nile appear regularly in art, television and film, covering all genres and ranging from classics such as George Bernard Shaw's *Caesar and Cleopatra* to the rather flippant *Cleopigtra, Queen of Denial* (*the Nile*), played by the most glamorous of actresses, Miss Piggy in episode 409 of *The Muppet Show*.

The ancient Egyptians themselves personified the Nile, or, more accurately, the Nile inundation as Hapy.[6] The start of the inundation was referred to as 'the arrival of Hapy'[7] and in the Egyptian language there is no word for 'inundation' other than his name, showing his importance. Hapy is represented in human form as a male with a large stomach and pendulous breasts, emphasising his androgyny as a fertility god (fig. 4). He is always shown with Nile plants upon his head and often bearing an offering tray with the produce of the Nile upon it. Although an important deity in the Egyptian pantheon, no temple was built for him and no priesthood worked on his behalf. Instead statues of the god appeared in most temples, often bearing the face of the current king. Offerings to Hapy were left at the caverns of the first cataract, thought to be his dwelling place, or thrown directly into the Nile. The most important time for giving offerings to Hapy was at the start of the inundation:

> When you overflow, O Hapy,
> Sacrifice is made for you;
> Oxen are slaughtered for you,
> A great oblation is made to you.
> Fowl is fattened for you,
> Desert game snared for you,
> As one repays your bounty.[8]

3 The Church of
Saint Sergius, Cairo

This personification led to representations in the nineteenth century portraying the mythical ritual of 'sacrificing a virgin to the god of the Nile', thought to appease the deity of the Nile, ensuring ample floods. However, this rite is not an ancient Egyptian one, and first appears in the Islamic text, *Marvels of Things Created and Miraculous Aspects of Things Existing* by al-Qazwīnī, Zakarīyā' ibn Muhammad (1685 CE). The ritual described took place in July in the seventh century CE, and comprised a virgin dressing in bridal clothes who was thrown to the goddess of the Nile. At the time, the Egyptian elders asked permission of the Muslim leader Amar bin Al-As to continue this ritual, but he banned it as being against Islam. This troubled the elders who claimed if the ritual was to be abandoned the Nile would not flood. Al-As did not allow the sacrifice and the inundation failed. By September, when the Nile still had not risen, Al-As reported the incident to Hadrat Umar who sent a card to him invoking the name of Allah and told him to throw the card into the river. He did this and the next morning the river rose to its full flood height, proving Allah could cause the river to flood with no need for ancient customs. The Egyptian elders were in awe and immediately converted to Islam.

It is clear this text was propaganda to explain how the conversion to Islam in Egypt was completed. At this point the ancient Egyptian religion was forgotten and any surviving rituals were extremely distorted.

The personification of the Nile is something that is also embedded in the Western myth of the river. One author personifies the flow of the river as a human lifespan: 'It leaves its boisterous youth behind in the gorges and canyons of the African mountains, its sulky adolescence in the swamps of the Sudan, and the growling protests of its middle age in the cataracts of Nubia. By the time it passed Aswan ... it has achieved the calm of old age.'[9]

In the 1990s an Ethiopian newspaper stated the Blue Nile, which joins the White Nile to form the Egyptian Nile, is accused of 'treachery, theft and robbery' due to the erosion and destruction it caused. An Ethiopian poet also used this theme in his work further accusing the river of arrogance, desertion and betrayal of its homeland and of causing the Ethiopians to die from drought and famine as it flows pointlessly into the sea.[10] Unfortunately, the river is unable to defend itself against such accusations, but is recognised as the giver of life which can be used in its defence. Hecataeus (sixth century BCE) praises the river: 'O generous Nile, you give life', and Herodotus, a century later, commented that Egypt 'was the gift of the Nile'. The ideas of personification are clearly diverse but have been present for centuries.

The ancient Egyptians believed the origin of the Nile was at the first cataract, with the caves serving as a residence for Hapy, under the protection of the god Khnum. Hapy was therefore primarily worshipped at the sites of Elephantine and Gebel el Silsila in this region. We know now that the origins of the Nile extend much further south, although this was not discovered until the mid-nineteenth century – the culmination of thousands of years of exploration. Herodotus

(480–425 BCE) speculated on the origins of the river but was unable to obtain any information regarding this or the inundation, and suggested that during the winter the sun was driven off its course by storms, and therefore the Nile had less water as there was no rain falling into it. He generally concluded the source was unknown.

Alexander the Great suggested the Ganges in India was one of the Nile tributaries,[11] and this was still considered possible as late as 1470 CE. The Greek geographer Ptolemy (83–161 CE) also speculated about the origins of the Nile and tried to locate it in the African heartland. In his *Geography* he traced the origin in the Mountains of the Moon, the great basin and the eastern tributaries. In 1436 CE the myth of the origins were recorded by an Italian traveller, Nicolo de'Conti, when a mission was organised to discover the Nile source by Prestor John, the Christian king of Abyssinia. He believed in order to discover the source it would be necessary to use a race of men who survived solely on fish. Therefore, he raised a group of babies with fish as their staple diet and when they grew to adulthood they went on the expedition, which led them to the Mountains of the Moon. Some men who explored the Nile pouring from the mountain did not return, while the others kept what they had seen a secret, maintaining the mystery of the Nile origins.[12]

4 Hapy the god of the inundation at Abu Simbel

The lack of understanding of the origins of the Nile led to myths as to how it flooded each year and the potential control the Egyptians held over it. The ancient Egyptians built this natural phenomenon into their mythology and recorded that the tears of Isis, cried over the body of her dead brother/husband Osiris, fell into the river, raising the waters.[13] The rising water saw the appearance of Hapy, who was greeted with great jubilation by the populous. The importance of this time of year is also emphasised in the Old Kingdom Pyramid Text (581), which specifies that the 'Meadows laugh, and the riverbanks are inundated'[14] showing the total reliance on the Nile by the living and the importance of the fertility and therefore rebirth of the dead in the underworld. The coming of the inundation was likened to the arrival of the dead king as Osiris in the afterlife.

Even once the traditional Egyptian religion disappeared, the inundation was still celebrated in Egypt. The Coptic Christians celebrated the rise of the Nile on the 'Night of the Drop' (17 June), believed to be when the archangel appeared to the Lord in order to raise the Nile.[15] The Muslims in Cairo also celebrated this day, referred to as *Munadee el-Nil* or the 'Herald of the Nile'. Once the High Dam was completed in 1971, the Nile no longer flooded although the celebrations were still performed.

Medieval Egyptians seemed to have no clearer understanding of the mystery of the inundation and the thirteenth-century chronicler Jean de Joinville commented: 'Nobody knows how these inundations occur unless it be by God's will … when morning comes, the Egyptians find in their nets, cast into the river products such as ginger, rhubarb, aloes and cinnamon.'[16]

Many medieval individuals believed that the source, and therefore the inundation, was controlled by Ethiopian emperors, and this idea was to dominate Eastern and European thought for over 500 years. There is no denying that Ethiopia and Egypt are linked by the Nile as well as social bonds. Ethiopia controlled the source of the Nile and the silt the Egyptians relied on, but as a Christian country Ethiopia relied on the Egyptian Coptic Church for the selection of their *abun* (patriarch), and viewed Egypt as a sacred land, a refuge of the holy family.[17] Even though, by the 1960s, the Egyptian authorities knew a great deal more about the source of the Nile and the workings of the river, they saw the building of the High Dam at Aswan as a psychological bid for freedom[18] from this potential threat from the Ethiopian emperor.

The mythologising of the Nile is a complex issue with many branches and variants, but ultimately it seems to stem from the ancient Egyptians themselves. However, even then there were conflicting ideas. The Egyptians were aware of their reliance on the Nile for their very existence, and as a riverine society many of their day-to-day activities were carried out on water. Many people, especially from the lower end of society, made a living from the river and without them the rest of society could not function. However, the elite members of the Egyptian society did not appreciate the work these people performed on the Nile and their plight is described in the Middle Kingdom *Satire of the Trades*:

> I'll speak of the fisherman also,
> His is the worst of all the jobs;
> He labours on the river,
> Mingling with crocodiles.
> When the time of reckoning comes,
> He is full of lamentations;
> He does not say 'there's a crocodile'
> Fear has made him blind.
> Coming from the flowing water
> He says 'mighty god'[19]

Although it is clear from this that those who worked on the Nile were not held in high esteem, the Nile itself was revered. The contrast between the reality of Nile living and the beauty of it is held by the same members of society then as now. The workers see the reality and the wealthy (the tourists) see the beauty and exoticism. This is a fundamental part of the myth of the Nile. It is viewed by different people as different things; by the rich it is a playground, for leaders and kings an instrument of politics, and for the poor it is seen as the source of hard work. Most people choose to believe an image of their own making as the 'reality' of the Nile.

So is the river Nile a god, personified as a man with pendulous breasts; a sacred waterway featuring in the lives of Moses and the holy family? Is it an exotic route for thousands of cruise boats from the time of Cleopatra to the modern day? Or merely part of the daily struggle to put food in hungry mouths? It is all of these things and none of them. It is only possible for an individual to experience one of these Niles – even though they may witness the others, they cannot truly experience them. For example, the rich Nile cruiser will witness the men fishing but will not understand the hardship of being a fisherman. They will witness the quaintness of the task almost as if they are actors there for their entertainment. The fisherman, on the other hand, may feel contempt for these idle cruisers, interfering with his daily routine, not realising that these people work hard when they are not on holiday. Everyone experiences the Nile differently and therefore will have a different idea of what the Nile means. Consequently there is not a *single* myth of the Nile but many, each varying according to the individual view-point, political or personal agenda.

2

AN ANCIENT RIVER STILL EVOLVING IN MANY WAYS

5000–3150 BCE

Egypt and her civilisation are relatively young in the history of the Nile, and it is only in the last 10,000 years that the river has prominently featured in the lives of the Egyptian people. The Nile was formed 160 million years ago when the tectonic plates shifted, and further shifts 25 million years ago created the Ethiopian mountains in the southern region of the continent. The Nile course as we know it was formed only 18,000 years ago due to the increased rainfall in the Ethiopian highlands, creating a flood plain and the Nile Valley. This highland rainfall caused the annual inundation and was fundamental to the fertility of the Nile Valley: 'an ancient river but one that is still evolving in many ways.'[1]

For the last 5000 years the fertile land surrounding the Nile covered an area of only 34,000km^2, and although the fertile land mass has not changed much in this time, its course has. The Nile is unusual as the discharge of a river is usually in proportion to the volume of the water catchment area, but the amount of water that reaches the Mediterranean is minimal as the flow ebbs substantially by the time it flows through the Delta.

The annual inundation was essential to many aspects of Egyptian civilisation; it dictated agricultural success, was incorporated into the religion, dictated when monumental building works were carried out and influenced the calendar, with New Year falling on the first day of the flood. The Nile rose at Aswan in June, never before 17 May or after 6 July, and surged in volume and speed for 100 days, reaching its maximum height in September. The water took twelve days to flow from Aswan to Cairo and six days to retreat,[2] and was a time of great concern for the Egyptians. If the water levels were too high, the land would be ruined, and if the water level was too low the land would not be fertilised. Both scenarios ended in failed crops, famine and death. From July until October the land was covered in water and the Egyptians could do nothing but wait for it to subside. During the pharaonic period idle farmers during these months were conscripted to help with the construction of royal monuments until they were needed to tend to the fields. From 1830 CE these annual floods were kept in check with a series of dams and sluices, and the High Dam at Aswan, opened in 1971, stopped the Nile flooding altogether, making a more stable environment but removing the one thing that had remained consistent throughout the history of Egypt.

So how has the Nile moulded the society that relied on it for survival? The answer is tied in with the ever-changing climate of Egypt. The climate prior to 5000 BCE was inconsistent, with periods of increased rainfall between 9200–6000 BCE and then again in 5000 BCE, and after a brief dry spell more rain in 4000 BCE. By 2350 BCE the climate had stabilised and was as arid as it is today.[3] During the wet spells the higher land was inhabited by elephants, giraffes, rhinoceroses, ostriches, wild asses, cattle, antelope, gazelle, ibex and deer, which could sustain a human population.

It is only in the last century that the concept of the pre-dynastic period has been understood. When Manetho devised his king list, his Old Kingdom began with the third dynasty, and this list and dynasty divisions were adopted by Egyptologists. In the last century excavations uncovered evidence of dynasties 0–2, which are now termed the early dynastic period with cultures older than that termed the pre-dynastic and the pre-historic. In 1894[4] at Koptos, El Ballas, and in 1895–1900[5] at Naqada, the first pre-dynastic material was discovered, believed to represent a foreign, rather than an earlier Egyptian, culture.[6] This theory of foreign infiltration dominated Egyptological debate until the 1960s, with Emery even suggesting the early dynastic culture was introduced by an Eastern 'master race'. As a similarity between this material and that found in the Near East was discovered, it was taken as evidence of mass migration. The popularity of this theory ignored the evidence of cultural development[7] and widespread distribution of material throughout Egypt.[8] The theory of mass invasion is no longer accepted, with continuity of culture between pre-dynastic and early dynastic society indicating they were the same people,[9] who, on the whole, developed independently of external influence.

Since the 1960s studies of the pre-dynastic and pre-historic have intensified, answering questions regarding the origins of the Egyptian civilisation. The Delta region in the north was always wetter than the rest of the country and prior to 5500 BCE it was probably swamp land, unsuited to settlements. Upper Egypt, therefore, has produced more evidence of Egypt's early inhabitants and their transition from hunter-gatherers to storers to sedentary society can be traced. The climatic changes greatly affected the lifestyle of the inhabitants of the Nile Valley, with arid periods affecting the fauna available for hunting. Communities were forced to move onto ever-decreasing areas of fertile land, as the desert slowly encroached upon the Nile Valley. As the climate continued to change, the early Egyptians were forced to clear the Savannah areas nearer the Nile, domesticating flora and fauna, although the fertile valley was narrower, providing less space for cultivation. The continuing expansion of the population eventually led to the unification of Egypt. This initial domestication of plants and animals was essential to the new semi-sedentary life. The earliest evidence, however, shows manipulation rather than full-domestication, although one soon led to the other.

The earliest domestication was in approximately 6000 BCE when millet was cultivated in the Dunqul Oasis, showing pockets of settled communities in this region at this time.[10] Badarian sites in particular show wild castor seeds were collected for production of oil, in addition to wheat, barley and flax, enabling production of linen. Evidence from Lower Egyptian Amratian sites show flax, lentils, peas, figs and berries were also present and, if not cultivated, were at least an aspect of their lifestyle and subsistence.[11] Studies indicate sheep, goats, dogs, cattle and pigs were domesticated during the Amratian and Gerzean periods,[12] raised for food, work and secondary products such as wool, milk and leather.[13]

The domestication of animals and development of permanent settlements saw the expansion of religious beliefs and ritualistic behaviour. Three burials from Toshka had bovid horns placed at the head of the deceased – perhaps an early association between rulers and cattle. Bull iconography has also been discovered at the later site of Merimda Beni Salama (c. 5000 BCE), in the form of the earliest sculptures in Egypt: anthropomorphic figures and fragments of bovid sculptures.[14] The remains of young cattle at Hierakonpolis (Gerzean) indicate cattle sacrifice may have taken place here.[15]

The domestication of plants and animals, and the ritual and practical associations also altered the utilisation of time as society adapted to the new lifestyle. Time was now spent on things other than food production, such as the production of luxury items. In 8000 BCE, the production of luxury pottery shows a more settled society, as they could be used for the duration of their stay and then discarded. As some of these vessels have diameters of more than 50cm they clearly would not be suitable for a transient society. This pottery, or coarse-ware, was decorated with incised wavy lines and geometric shapes, and was used primarily for cooking. During the Amratian period new highly polished black-topped B-Ware was introduced (fig. 5). These vessels were labour intensive, showing not only a developed skill but also a hierarchical society where time could be spent on non-essential items, and ownership was a sign of status.

This newly developed, stratified, settled society is known as the pre-dynastic period. The pre-dynastic period began with an arid spell between 6000-5500 BCE and more people were forced to leave the encroaching desert area for the lush Nile

Valley. The earliest settled societies are located in the Fayum in the north, with evidence of two cultures: the Fayum B (6000 BCE) and Fayum A (5000 BCE).[16] The material culture of the Fayum A people shows there are some connections with the Levantine coastal regions, indicative of a transient society, further supported by the lack of houses at the main sites of this culture.[17] The sites show evidence of hearths, grain silos and depressions for sunken pots used for storage of emmer wheat and barley. This is the first evidence of cultivated agriculture and suggests that the Fayum cultures supplemented their hunter-gatherer lifestyle with domesticated plants. The silos and hearths were situated on naturally elevated land and were maintained all year round. At the same time the domestication of goats, sheep and dogs was taking place. The climate at this time had entered a humid phase, resulting in a higher water table, flooding of the Fayum lake[18] and an abundance of fish. Both the Nile perch, which favoured deep waters, and the catfish, which favoured shallower waters, were caught, showing different fishing skills in use. Studies of the growth rings of the catfish have identified they were caught in the summer, as they wallowed in the shallow waters making them easy to catch, and at the end of summer when they laid their eggs and congregated in the same place.[19]

The Fayum was a key site and seemed to form the intersection between the eastern Sahara, the Near East and the Nile Valley,[20] and studies of the flint workmanship of the Fayum cultures show they may have spread from lithic centres in the Congo or western Sudan, indicating a movement of people from these areas northwards throughout Egypt.[21] There were also a number of imported Palestinian pottery types here suggesting that they were trading or travelling to the region and showing a major development of this community.[22] Unlike the later Badarian culture, the Fayum A and B people survived primarily on their hunting and fishing skills, rather than domestication of plants and animals, which was used more as a supplement to their diet rather than as a staple.[23]

The main site for the Badarian culture was El Badari, near Asyut, although they were a semi-sedentary society with no permanent settlements and the evidence intimates they lived in temporary shelters made of skin draped over poles. These temporary settlements contained small animal enclosures, showing seasonal domestication (fig. 6), by plucking a small number of cattle from a larger herd, domesticating it for milk, meat and leather.[24] The faunal remains from the Badarian sites reveal their diet consisted of hippopotamuses, antelope and gazelle – all products of seasonal hunting. The additional subsistence from seasonal domestication and farming suited the newly developed arid climate, and basket-lined grain pits at El-Mostagedda were used for storing emmer and barley during the dry season.[25]

Cemeteries outside the settlement boundaries comprised small units of approximately 30 graves, either representative of small social units or, more likely,

5 Naqada I B-Ware. (*Courtesy of UCL, Petrie Museum of Egyptian Archaeology* UC5685)

6 Model cattle from a Naqada II burial. British Museum

of the short period of habitation at the site.[26] The bodies were wrapped in baskets or animal skins with the head in the south facing west,[27] often with the hands cupping the face.[28] These burials contained a number of grave goods including stone palettes, ivory spoons, combs, stone vases and clay figurines, indicative of a hierarchical society. Other burials contained beads of cornelian, jasper, alabaster, steatite, diorite, amazonite and serpentine, (fig. 7) all imported from the eastern desert in the region of the Red Sea, showing they were expensive and therefore highly valued. The discovery of Amratian rock art along the Wadi Hamammat route to the Red Sea shows it was used throughout the pre-dynastic period. Discovery of copper, turquoise, steatite, pine and cedar at Badarian sites shows further trade routes existed with Palestine, Sinai and Syria.[29] The quantity of such goods indicate these expeditions or exchange networks were regular yet small scale events,[30] asserting that the Badarian community was an organised, stratified society. This is supported by a number of male graves containing anklets, bracelets, necklaces, girdles[31] and cosmetics of malachite (from the eastern desert), galena (from the Red Sea) and ochre (locally mined),[32] crushed on palettes of stone, mined in the Sinai. As imported minerals, the use of cosmetics was a further indication of wealth and status, as was the general adornment of the body with jewellery. The more elaborate the jewellery, and the more exotic the cosmetics, the wealthier the individual. The Amratian period saw increased numbers of cosmetic items included amongst burial goods, and although portable, may have originated during the time of hunter-gatherers, developing into items of public display. Petrie, using anthropological evidence, asserted that Egyptians used black eye paint to protect their eyes from the sun in the same manner that the Inuits did.[33] The Badarian material culture, although contemporary with the Fayum A and B cultures of the north, was far in advance of them, with finer detail, superior craftsmanship and greater aestheticism,[34] although this was to be superseded by the Naqada culture.

Naqada was one of the largest pre-dynastic sites in Egypt, on the west bank of the Nile approximately 26km north of Luxor. This culture gradually spread throughout Egypt, from Khartoum to the Delta, producing an almost homogenous society.[35] The culture of Naqada ran smoothly from I (Amratian) into II (Gerzean) and III (early dynastic period), showing cultural continuity between the pre-dynastic and dynastic cultures. At Naqada over 2000 graves were discovered, indicating this must have been the administrative centre.[36] The main difference between the Badarian and the Amratian period is the inclusion of decorated objects in burials, not only pottery but also cosmetic implements of ivory and bone bearing complex images of animals and humans.[37] The importance of Naqada continued until the early dynastic period when it was used for royal burials.

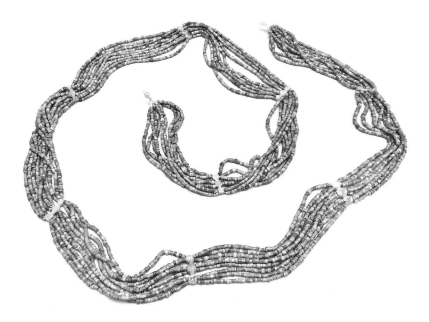

7 Badarian Lapis necklace from Mostagedda. British Museum

Hierakonpolis, on the west bank of the Nile, 113km north of Aswan, was the largest settlement and cemetery from the Amratian and Gerzean period and it is estimated that thousands of burials originally took place here. Child burials included funerary goods with prestige items such as ivory, lapis lazuli, copper, silver and gold, indicative of inherited status.[38] The settlement at Hierakonpolis bears similarity to the other sites of the period in Middle and Upper Egypt, although burial goods demonstrate long-distant trade, with a social hierarchy based on luxury goods.[39] In the Gerzean period this international trade increased with the introduction of a donkey route through the Sinai, although the river was essential as it provided access to all trade routes.

The Gerzean period saw a mass migration towards the flood plain at Hierakonpolis, with enclosures employed as craft centres for lithic, bead and vessel manufacture, although the absence of finished objects at the site indicates that they were removed and used or sold elsewhere. Many of the goods seem to have been created purely for the grave[40] and were never utilised in life, showing an increase in non-essential craft manufacture. This would take the craftsmen away from food production, suggesting the start of an elite class. This period saw the introduction of decorated D-Ware pottery, bearing images in red ochre, of boats, landscape, flora, fauna and humans (fig. 8). These figures include females with raised arms (fig. 9), associated with an early bovine cult, and have also been discovered as figures in

8 Naqada II D-Ware pottery. (*Courtesy of UCL, Petrie Museum of Egyptian Archaeology UC10769*)

the round. These females are often accompanied by smaller images of men wearing penis sheaths, leather examples of which have been discovered in burials in Naga-ed-Deir and Hierakonpolis. This pottery was fired at a higher temperature than the earlier types and required the building of enclosed kilns – a time-consuming job. The images were essential to the function of these vessels as they were painted before they were fired and they emphasise the importance of the landscape, the river in particular, as most of them are decorated with images of boats with oars[41] and small cabins on the deck (fig. 10). Riverine travel was obviously essential to this newly stratified society and the human figures represent some aspect of their social hierarchy.

Hierakonpolis was also favoured by royal patronage and the now lost Tomb 100 (fig. 11), a large subterranean tomb with internal plastered walls, was painted with polychromatic scenes. This was not the only tomb of this size at Hierakonpolis, and it was discovered in the centre of a cemetery of approximately 150 smaller burials. This was the earliest decorated tomb in Egypt and shows a number of images later incorporated into the dynastic artistic canon. The tomb is particularly important as it is the first example of artwork created purely for the tomb and is evident of ritualistic adoption, political and social change in Egypt.[42]

9 Gerzean female figurine with arms raised.
Ashmoleon Museum, Oxford

10 Naqada II D-Ware
pottery. (*Courtesy of UCL,
Petrie Museum of Egyptian
Archaeology UC13511*)

Religious developments can be identified in the ritual burial practices of these early cultures. Burials at a number of Gerzean Upper Egyptian sites demonstrate the practice of dismemberment and removal of body parts from the graves; a burial at El-Amra is of a dismembered body with the leg bones separated from the torso and arranged alongside fish-tailed flint knives, a diorite mace-head and a fish-tailed cosmetic palette.[43] At Naqada three graves had the skull replaced with another object, including vessels and an ostrich egg incised with small figures. Other internments had the skull placed on top of a pile of stones or mud-brick, or between the legs or feet. Other burials were minus the arms and hands, and one had the hands placed beneath the skull.[44] There were two cases of complete dismemberment, where the bones were placed together in a pattern; one had the legs of four bodies placed parallel to each other and another had a pile of pelvis bones with the leg bones in the corner of the grave, the ribs surrounding the vertebrae and the arm bones in the middle, showing an amount of creativity in the organisation of the remains. One multiple burial comprising a large pile of disjointed bones displayed signs of teeth marks, and Petrie commented that the ends of some of the bones were broken and the marrow removed.

These practices were not widespread, but equally not rare for the period, and displayed an interest in the body after death. Excavations at Hierakonpolis (Naqada II) emphasise this, as some burials show early attempts at preserving the body – a precursor for mummification. Many of the bodies were wrapped in linen shrouds or placed within a leather sack, but there were some in which the head and hands were wrapped in layers of linen dipped in resin. Some areas of the body were padded out with linen before the final wrappings were arranged, with layers of bandages up to 10cm thick.[45] The bodies were then covered in coarse linen shrouds. Whether they were attempting to preserve the body is not certain. Resin was an important element of this early wrapping and pellets of it were buried as grave goods, and one body at Hierakonpolis was completely wrapped in frankincense bark. Was the resin being used as a preservative or did it have another ritual association?

These changes in burial practices reflect changing attitudes to the dead and, by extension, themselves as a community (fig. 12). It is possible that the dismemberment of the bodies enabled them to be distributed over a wider area, perhaps as an increased desire for commemoration.[46] It has been suggested this commemoration of the dead was a way of mourning the passing of the individual as well as losing a piece of personal history, acknowledging a new widespread social awareness. The dismemberment of the bodies was labour intensive and required protracted exposure of the body after death. Petrie associated this with the mythology of Osiris and Seth, where the body of Osiris was cut into 14 pieces and scattered throughout Egypt. Although there is no way of knowing whether there is a connection between the two, there were clearly ritualistic associations with the burials, and in some of the burials at Hierakonpolis large conical jars filled with ashes, thought to have been from hearths associated with funerary rituals and the preparation of the funerary goods and food, were also buried.[47] The dismemberment of the bodies and the early attempts at mummification were a way of creating an image out of the deceased, which may be a precursor to the idea of the semi-deification of the dead.

11 Reconstruction of tomb 100, Ashmoleon Museum. (*Courtesy of Brian Billington*)

The Egyptian culture continued to develop until the Naqada III or the early dynastic period, which saw the foundation of all aspects of dynastic Egyptian culture. However, it is clear the Egyptian civilisation started out as a number of isolated tribes settling in the Nile Valley due to climatic change causing deterioration of flora and fauna upon which they had previously relied. They were forced to move closer to the river and learn how to manipulate their environment and then to tame it through domestication of plants and animals. The now arid climate meant the newly sedentary societies were totally dependent on the Nile and its annual cycle. Through manipulation of the river, its wildlife and its flooding, they were able to develop a complex culture which remained strong and dynamic for a further 3000 years.

12 The Gerzean burial of Ginger. British Museum

3

CIVILISATION
WITHOUT CITIES

3150–2613 BCE

Many widely accepted theories regarding the formation of the central-ised state can be traced back to Manetho's record which claims it began with the unification of Upper and Lower Egypt by King Narmer or Menes, in approximately 3100 BCE. The archaeological evidence tells a different story, indicating that the formation of the state was not the result of a single event, but a slow period of development where the foundations of kingship, religion, funerary beliefs and administration were formed. The gradual development of the unified state may have grown from the need to utilise the Nile for survival, and the organisation of people to build, maintain and protect earthworks required a centralised leader. Once these structures were in place the wider centralised government came into being,[1] as one ruler slowly took over smaller city states. This pre-occupation with the control of the flood is apparent as all kings are presented in acts of irrigation (fig. 13),[2] and the Old Kingdom represented the importance of this by incorporating it into the mythology surrounding the first king of the gods, Osiris, who taught the world how to irrigate the land and farm.

During the Naqada III period the beginnings of such a centralised administration is identified, as it was a time of localised unification and of the foundation of a hierarchical society. This was instigated initially by the domestication of plants and animals, with groups working and living on the same land for a set period of time. The cultivation of land destroyed the already diminishing savannah-like environment, depleting the numbers of large mammals, such as elephants, rhinoceroses, buffalo and larger types of antelope.[3] The savannah landscape was slow to return, resulting in conflicts over territory and natural resources, the development of personal ambition and the desire to produce agricultural surplus to exchange or to lead a better life than others in the community. From these beginnings a

13 Ramses III participating in agricultural activity at Medinet Habu

leader emerged: the strongest or richest, responsible for controlling and over-
seeing the irrigation projects.[4] These small settlements eventually merged into
villages, under a local leader. The development of such a hierarchical society ran
parallel with the development of religion and ideology displayed through burial
and the associated grave goods.

The southern Naqada culture was dominant in Egypt and expanded, absorbing
the northern Maadian culture which comprised of agriculturalists, situated in a
buffer zone between Egypt and the eastern trade route towards the Levant. This
was particularly lucrative and was therefore an important area to control.[5] Evidence
from Maadi indicates they were trading with the Levant before the Naqada III
culture reached them, and six stone-built structures at Maadi, up to 2.5m deep into
the natural rock containing evidence of habitation including ash, limestone spindle
whorls, worked animal bone and flint knives, are thought to be Levantine in origin.
These structures have been interpreted as features to counteract the desert heat,

storage facilities or possibly defensive buildings.[6] Some have gone so far as to suggest these subterranean structures were a 'foreign quarter'[7] as numerous Palestinian vessels and Levantine flint tools have been found here.

Trade during the pre-dynastic period was primarily with the East. Naqada II tombs have contained lapis lazuli mined principally from Badakhshan on the borders of Afghanistan and Pakistan, although a further source has been identified near Quetta, which may have been easier to reach from Egypt.[8] Tomb U-j at Abydos, which comprises 12 rooms covering 66.4m²,[9] in addition to many bone, ivory and pottery artefacts, has 400 Palestinian jars which originally contained imported wine.[10] The content of the jars is known to be wine due to the remains of grape pips, salt of tartaric acid, terebinth and stringed fig slices found within them.[11] Grapes are native to the Levant, whereas the wine-making industry in Egypt did not start until dynasty 0, indicating they were imported, although the clay seals are Egyptian, which shows a centralised control of imported goods.[12]

Other evidence of Palestineian imports were found at the entrance ramp to the tomb of Semekhet, which was saturated up to 3ft deep with aromatic oil and even after 5000 years the scent was still strong. Thirty labelled vessels from the tomb of Qa'a, from the end of the first dynasty, describe the importation of oil made from berries and tree resins from Syria-Palestine.[13] The majority of evidence of imported goods comes from funerary contexts, which by the end of Naqada II contained display-oriented material goods, buried as a sign of status. This material culture saw an increase in importation and trade with the Levant and the East, facilitated by an improvement in the transportation system and by the early dynastic period a caravan route ran north-eastwards out of Egypt, circling Sinai, and along the coastline to the eastern Mediterranean. This route linked three other routes from Sumerian cities, crossing western Iraq, Jordon and Syria[14] which increased the imported goods available. This increased trade saw mass production of new crafts as well as improved transport, including the pack donkey, and river and sea-going vessels facilitating long-distance exchanges.[15] The majority of this travel, whether for trade purposes or to aid the Naqada III population with their expansion throughout Egypt, would have been impossible without the river Nile and the extensive use of boats. The larger boats required long timber planks which were unavailable in Egypt, so instead they built their boats of cedar from Byblos,[16] indicative of a healthy trade relationship. Woods native to Egypt were acacia, sycamore and persea, with acacia being the only one suitable for boat building.[17]

By the Negada II period (Gerzean) rock art and pottery decoration included regular images of boats and cattle, reflecting the lifestyle change that occurred throughout the Nile Valley. The decoration on D-Ware pottery is invariably representative of the landscape, including water, trees, mountains and local fauna.

The boats pictured encompass numerous oars and a single structure on the deck, similar to the later shrines on sacred barques, which are thought to have accommodated the chieftains whilst sailing down the Nile or the mummy when used as a funerary barge. Similar boats are depicted in Tomb 100 from Hierakonpolis, and are associated with a funerary procession. The boats of this period were possibly seagoing craft as they bear a similarity to those represented in the rock art of the Wadi Hammamat, along the route to the Red Sea. The boat styles themselves were Mesopotamian in type, with high prows and sterns, and it is clear they had contact with the Naqada II Egyptians.

Numerous real and model boats have been found from the early dynastic period and they were closely associated with the burials of kings and high officials. Tomb 3357 in Saqqara, thought originally to belong to Hor-Aha (first dynasty), had to the north side of the structure a boat pit, complete with a wooden solar boat. At Abydos the 12 boat burials south-east of Djer's funerary enclosure contained wooden hulls of boats 18–21m long but only 50cm high, with a mudbrick structured encasing them. Pottery discovered within the boats dates to the early dynastic period but it is uncertain from which dynasty. The boats were obviously intended for use in the afterlife, with boulders to use as anchors included. Most boats in Egypt would not have a use for anchors (as they could be moored along the river bank each evening),[18] only sea-bound vessels required one.

The purpose of such boat burials is uncertain, although it is commonly accepted that they formed part of the funerary entourage or represented lunar, solar or stellar barques for the deceased to travel across the nocturnal sky[19] accompanied by the gods. The Abydos boats are the earliest association with the king.[20] The only boat from one of these boat pits to be reconstructed was that of Khufu. There were five pits in total,[21] two containing boats, one in good enough condition to be rebuilt while the other had been damaged by damp and termites. Regardless of the function of these boat burials, there was obviously an important connection between royalty and boats, with a ceremonial use for the Nile itself.

Other ideologies of kingship can be traced to the Narmer Palette (fig. 14), which represents the king on one side wearing the white crown (hedjet) of Upper Egypt in the traditional smiting pose, arm raised holding a mace poised to hit a kneeling enemy with hieroglyphs behind him reading the 'place of the harpoon', which was the sixth Lower Egyptian nome. Above the enemy is the land hieroglyph, representative of the Delta, bearing the head of a captive enemy facing the king.[22] Beneath the king's feet are two fallen enemies, followed by his sandal and seal bearer with a cylinder seal around his neck, emphasising the importance of administration in early kingship. This scene is often taken to show the violent takeover of the north by Narmer, a southern ruler, as on the recto of the palette the king is in procession wearing the red crown (deshret) of Lower Egypt, walking towards the hieroglyphics for 'Great Gate of Horus, the harpooner', which could be Buto.[23] However, archaeological evidence suggests that an event like this did not occur as recorded, although as conquered enemies feature prominently, warfare was evidently an important part of the unification process and the early dynastic period.[24] From Naqada II onwards the gradual unification of Egypt took place with the north assimilating into the south, resulting in small skirmishes[25] rather than a single battle.

It is quite probable, however, that by the time Narmer came to the throne Egypt was already a unified land, as it was for Scorpion who ruled before him. This is evident from the Scorpion mace-head[26] (plate 3), discovered alongside the Narmer Palette in Hierakonpolis which shows the king wearing a ceremonial bull's tail and the tall white conical crown of Upper Egypt, demonstrating his control over the south. The king is holding a hoe in his hands and it is thought that he is either digging irrigation dykes, laying the foundations of a temple or the enclosure wall of a settlement. Although we do not know exactly what this scene represents, the imagery was repeated for a further 3000 years as an important element of kingship ideology.

14 Facsimile of the Narmer Palette in Royal Ontario Museum. (*Courtesy of Public Domain on Wikicommons*)

15 Hunter's Palette.
British Museum

According to Herodotus the first king of the dynastic period was Menes, lead-ing many to debate as to his identity: 'The priests told me that it was Men, the first king of Egypt, who raised the dam which protects Memphis from the floods.'[27]

Generally, Menes is associated with either Narmer or Scorpion, as the first named rulers of dynasty 0, but the hieroglyphic sign for 'mn' has been found on numerous labels of King Hor-Aha, the successor of Narmer, providing a strong case in favour of Menes and Hor-Aha being one and the same.[28] Menes was accredited with two important roles of the king: one, the construction of a cen-tralised city and, two, the water management system employed with which to do it. It was once said that early Egypt was 'a civilisation without cities', but the foundation of Memphis in 3100 BCE, which maintained its status as a capital city until the late period, shows this was not the case.[29] The effort engaged to build Memphis shows its importance in the foundation of a centralised government. Recent studies show the Nile has been slowly migrating eastwards since this period, making it possible that Memphis was built on reclaimed land. It is clear from excavations that by the early dynastic period basin irrigation expanded the amount of cultivated land and salination did not occur due to the annual floods flushing away the salts.[30] The ability to regulate the period of soil irrigation and increasing yield despite the difficult-to-work soil saw the introduction of hoes and ox-drawn ploughs, making the work easier[31] and more reliable, replacing hunting as a method of food production. Hunting activities were now practised by the elite as a sports pastime rather than a necessity (fig. 15).[32] Although basin irrigation was best managed at a localised level, due to the changing society with the elite relying on the food-producers, such irrigation was overseen locally but controlled centrally, ensuring sufficient surplus was produced.

Before the unification, there were important administrative centres in both the north and south of Egypt: Buto and Maadi in the north and Naqada, Abydos and Hierakonpolis in the south. Each city had their respective religious cults and practices which even after unification were maintained and incorporated into the ever-growing pantheon of the dynastic period. Until relatively recently, a great deal of our information about this period came from the Palermo Stone – annals listing the deeds of all kings from the pre-dynastic period to the fifth dynasty. It is recorded that the gods initially ruled Egypt, followed by demigods known as 'the Followers of Horus', who could be kings of the late pre-dynastic period[33] from the city of Hierakonpolis.

The connection between Horus and the king has been present since the earliest of times and the first royal names were written in a *serekh*[34] surmounted by Horus (fig. 16).[35] The absorption of the northern culture by the south saw the rivalry between the Followers of Horus and Seth which was to form the foundation of kingship ideology of later dynasties. Initially in the early pre-dynastic, Seth was the god of the south and Horus the god of the north, but by the early dynastic period these were reversed, with Horus worshipped at Hierakonpolis and Seth at Buto.

16 *Serekh* of Hor Aha.
British Museum

The mythology describes Horus conquering Seth, showing the south's dominance over the north.[36] The rivalry between the north and south continued for many years and the fourth king of the second dynasty, Sekhemib who reigned for 17 years, clearly supported the north as he changed his name to Seth-Peribsen and, instead of having an image of Horus on top of his *serekh* frame, he had an image of Seth. When Khasekhemwy took over the throne, the conflict continued and an inscription on a vase refers to 'the year of fighting the northern enemy within the city of Nekheb'. Nekheb (El Kab) was situated on the opposite side of the Nile to Nekhen (Hierakonpolis). The conflict must have been quite intense for the northern kings to reach this far south. A statue base of Khasekhemwy records that 47,209 northerners were killed in this conflict. A rudimentary peace ensued and Khasekhemwy, the final king of the second dynasty, married a northern princess to cement the alliance. She was called Nemathap and held the title of 'The King-Bearing Mother', and was later seen as the ancestress of the third dynasty.[37]

Other early dynastic cults were also absorbed into the later pantheon. For example, during the first dynasty, fish were an important element of ritual life, especially the Nile perch. They were represented in art and many cosmetic palettes were carved into fish shapes. The tomb of Narmer at Abydos included a number of fish models.[38] By the end of the Old Kingdom the catfish was considered sacred to Osiris and a sign of fertility. Other animals at this time had divine attributes: scorpions, lions, bulls, falcons, ibexes, gazelles and hounds, which are depicted as personifications of gods helping the king defeat his enemies or conduct rituals of state. The catfish, because of its habitation in the mud, was believed to guide the barque of Re through his nocturnal journey and catfish headed demons were depicted pulling the solar barque on its path through the night.[39] The people of Egypt relied on the power of animals during this time of early settlements, and the early kings even named themselves after such creatures,[40] such as Narmer (Catfish) and Scorpion, perhaps to adopt similar characteristics.[41]

Gods, other than animal deities were worshipped, and the earliest colossal statue was of Min of Koptos (fig. 17). The statue stands 4m tall, (13ft) is cylindrical in shape, with a huge phallus and a bearded face. A sash hangs from his waist bearing hieroglyphics of shells, an elephant, a stag's head, a swordfish, an hyena and an ox, similar to the rock art images of the period.[42] Further examination of these signs show Narmer's name is there, dating the statue as dynasty 0. Although the artistic style shows little resemblance to the later Egyptian canon, the characteristics of Min remained the same. This statue no doubt held an important place within a temple dedicated to Min at the site, although no such structure has been discovered. The quarrying, carving and erection of a statue of such scale demonstrates an organisation of society and community spirit,[43] as well as a perceived need for such a monument for ritual purpose.

17 The Colossal statue of Min from Koptos.
Ashmoleon Museum

The establishment of such ritual objects saw the development of sacred places, which can be traced to the early dynastic period and the location of royal burials. The most important burial site of the pre-dynastic and early dynastic period was Abydos, which was clearly viewed as a sacred place, although the reasons why are not clear. It is not until the end of the Old Kingdom that the site was identified with Upper Egyptian god Khentimentiu, who had a temple here, and Wepwawet. Khentimentiu was one of the later titles of Osiris, and the site of Abydos was believed to be Osiris' burial place and the location of his dismemberment by Seth. How much of this developed from pre-dynastic dismemberment practices is unknown.[44] However, the site of Abydos was used for royal burials from the Naqada III period onwards and all of the early rulers are represented here, showing a sequence of kings: Iry-Hor, Ka, Narmer and Aha.[45] These tombs can be used to identify not only the burial practices of the earliest kings, but also the development of kingship ideology, international relations and religious beliefs and practices. The monumental funerary structures show a political order unlike anything from the pre-dynastic period.[46]

The successor of Hor-Aha, Djer, had the largest tomb complex at Abydos with his burial chamber in the centre, where Petrie discovered a linen-wrapped arm with bracelets from the original burial.[47] The bracelets were kept but the arm was discarded and now all that remains are a few pieces of linen wrappings, some of which are in the Petrie Museum, London. Also surrounding the tomb of Djer were over 3000 satellite burials of servants who had gone to the grave with him. The tomb of his predecessor, Hor-Aha also shows traces of large wooden shrines in three chambers within the tomb and 33 satellite burials, all young males 20–25 years old. Near one of these satellite burials were the burials of seven young lions,[48] also put to death. The lions had long been associated with the king as well as royal and divine strength, and the capture and slaughter of such beasts further emphasised the strength of the king. The tomb of Qa'a, the last king of the first dynasty, at Abydos was small in comparison, standing only 30 x 23m and accompanied by 26 satellite burials. This early dynastic period is the only one where servants were sacrificed upon the death of the king, and research carried out by Nancy Lovell on the skeletons has shown that they died by strangulation.[49] Many of these satellite burials are accompanied by grave goods and stelae carved with their names, ensuring them a place in the afterlife. This practice of sacrificial burials stopped during the reign of Qa'a (c.2890 BCE) to be replaced in the dynastic period with servant statues and shabti figures. The very existence of such vast numbers of disposable servants makes it clear that a stratified society was firmly established.

The key settlements of the late pre-dynastic period were strategically placed along the eastern desert, where resources such as stone and gold were obtained. The city of Naqada itself was known in ancient Egypt as Nubt, which means 'Gold', indicative of the craft carried out here.[50] It was really these new-found crafts which separated the Naqada III culture from the earlier ones, the majority of which were for non-essential elite products. Hunter-gatherer societies rely on everyone helping with food production, whether it be hunting, gathering and later agriculture and food preparation, whereas the late pre-dynastic took people away from food production into craft production. This meant that the food producers were now producing food for the non-food producers, who were in turn producing objects for the elite. The non-food producers now relied on food producers to feed them; creating a hierarchy with the food producers at the bottom of the social scale. In order to finance the element of society that was not contributing to food production, taxes were introduced.[51]

Standard measures were developed to measure the harvest yield and therefore set the tax due. Further sets of measurements were also devised in order to accurately measure the agricultural boundaries, which were washed away each year by the floods. This meant strict records were kept of land distribution and annual yield. In order to pay the taxes it was essential for food producers to produce excess goods (foods, stone and raw materials),[52] which saw a rapid increase in food production.

The new crafts were not only non-essential, but also time consuming. The pre-dynastic cultures were exceptionally skilled with stonecraft, as can be identified by the stone palettes where often the carvings are in raised relief; difficult to execute using such basic tools. They were also adept at working hard stones such as granite and porphyry as well as soft stones like limestone and alabaster. As the demand for stone objects and vessels developed, for day-to-day life as well as status grave items, the search for raw materials became essential and replaced hunting for non-food producers. Gold and ivory were obtained from the south, stone and copper from the Near East, lapis lazuli from Afghanistan and obsidian from further afield. The final objects were destined for elite members of society and therefore they controlled the raw materials, manufacture, finished products and their distribution. This saw the establishment of a craftsmen class, who worked and started to live together.[53] The organisation of the craftsmen required a centralised administration which was regional initially and then national, instigated by a record-keeping system that began with the introduction of seal-making and the emergence of a rudimentary writing system.

Academic debate has argued that the earliest writing in Egypt was concerned with ceremonial aspects rather than administrative, and the Narmer palette is often stated as the first written record of an historical event. However, writing can be identified from the Gerzean period (Naqada II), predating political unification and the dynastic period, from bone labels in tomb U-j at Abydos, bearing numbers and a combination of up to four signs. These have been interpreted as being either sizes of cloth or records of the provenance of certain elite commodities. The tomb belonged to a local chief, and the signs include a throne and palace facade niching, which was further imbedded into the writing system in the form of the *serekh*, framing the king's Horus name, the first element of the royal titulary. The first king to have his name written in a *serekh* was Ka, although the symbol appeared on pottery from the start of Naqada III, probably naming the pot owner or provenance of the contents.[54]

Gerzean period pot marks provide evidence of early writing, although as the marks are quite primitive in nature some argue they cannot be considered writing.[55] It is believed that those signs incised on the pots before firing were potters marks and those incised after they were fired were the owner's marks,[56] or they were comparative to modern hallmarks where each sign communicates information, possibly about the contents of the container. These pot marks may be part of a centralised system, indicating they were widely understood, perhaps evidence of the beginnings of a central administration responsible for the distribution of labelled commodities, such as oil and imported wine.[57] It appears that the early use of writing, whilst often having a royal context, was employed primarily for economic and administrative purposes[58] within an elite social sphere.

Some of these early royal commodity labels are placed in registers like later text, although they are written using a primitive form of hieroglyphs, and the meanings are obscure. As the society developed and became more organised so did their artwork and written texts. The use of registers became common and by the end of the second dynasty they were an essential part of the Egyptian artistic and written canon. Record keeping continued to develop and by the reign of Den the sign for regnal year was introduced, indicating that royal annals were being kept.[59] Although now within the royal sphere, the recording of dates was still primarily for accounting. An ivory label from Abydos, probably affixed to a pair of sandals, records 'the first time of the smiting of the East', depicting Den with a mace raised above his head in a typical smiting scene, clubbing a foreign chieftain.

The development of the written language was concurrent with the spread of the Naqada II and III culture, which was aided by an elaborate state administration managed by such seals and tags. Once the culture spread, conscription was probably used for some of the monumental structures of the early dynasties. In order to organise such conscription, whether for building works or military expeditions, a developed writing system was required. Although the evidence from the early dynastic period is only in the form of labels and administrative items, later period copies of a surgical papyrus and the Memphite theology from the Shabaka Stone are said to have been originally written in the first dynasty,[60] although this is difficult to ascertain without further evidence of literary ability from this period.

The origins of the written language are often debated and similarities have been discovered between the Sumerian and Egyptian languages. Others believe the language was introduced from Mesopotamia,[61] although the connections with Sumerian are more pronounced, and some words such as hoe, spade, plough, corn, beer and carpenter are of Sumerian origin.[62] As these words are all related to trades it could suggest origins for these crafts in addition to language. The contact between the Egyptians and the Near East are attested from the Badarian period onwards and their influences are clear. Images such as the serpent-necked felines, a favourite theme of artists in Uruk, appear on one side of the Oxford palette and the Narmer palette. Although the design may have originated in Uruk, the meaning and ideology represented in the Egyptian examples were unique to Egypt, associated with the king's power to control chaotic forces.

By the end of the second dynasty, Egyptian civilisation had evolved into a hierarchical, highly organised, unified state. With the introduction of a writing system, they opened their world up to outsiders, creating standardised religious dogma, laws, administration, taxes, construction and warfare. All of these became clearer and more complex as the Old Kingdom began.

4

THE DESERT IS DYING
OF HUNGER

2498–1570 BCE

Changes in the habitat played a key role in the further development of the Old Kingdom civilisation, with the main focus of the centralised state being control and manipulation of the environment. Some believe the continuing development of the unified state was the result of communal water control in particular.[1] As the nature of the river and the Nile Valley left little option but to build settlements, agricultural buildings and storage facilities on mounds above the flood plain,[2] water management in such confined areas was essential to accommodate the expanding population, which in the Old Kingdom stood between 60,000 and 96,000 people.[3]

Evidence of government structure is scarce, with studies of cemeteries and titles being the only evidence of the administrative system. It seems the positions of power were given to those closest to the king. The closer to the royal burial a tomb was, the more important the person. Should an official possess a tomb in a royal cemetery such as Memphis, this was only at the behest of the king demonstrating their revered status. These elite relied heavily on the king both in life and death for their position.

There was a complex system of local administrators responsible for the day-to-day running of Egypt. The most important title was the local mayor (*haty*), responsible for law and order within his town, conscription of men for military exhibitions and building works, as well as land division and control, and localised water management. These local mayors descended from important families and were chosen for wisdom, courage and fairness.[4] There was no police force in the Old Kingdom and all law enforcement was carried out locally by the mayor and his peers. The legal system was centred on the concept of Maat, and often a 'Priest of Maat' resided over the court ensuring justice prevailed, although the decisions were made via a council.

In order for localised mayors to be centrally managed, nomes (provinces) were introduced. By the Middle Kingdom there were 42 nomes; 22 in Upper Egypt and 20 in Lower Egypt. Each nome was governed by a nomarch, who answered to the central government. Each had a system of internal control, a capital city, practices, gods and religious laws, although they were ultimately under the control of the king. Each nome was required to pay taxes to the king and Old Kingdom tombs show processions of offering bearers, representing the villages, manors and estates controlled by the tomb owner.[5] The calculation of pre-defined taxes led to the introduction of measurement systems and advancement in astronomy to predict the rise of the inundation and the expected volume of crops.[6] Local mayors were responsible for ensuring fields were suitably irrigated in order to make the tax payments. With such a locally governed society, a new sense of patriotism arose within the local community and many autobiographies start with the phrase: 'I have come from my town! I have descended from my province.'

This love of home was maintained for the remainder of the dynastic period and a common greeting was 'may you die in your town'. Soldiers and merchants also expressed the desire to die and be buried at home rather than in chaotic places outside of its borders. The most important town was Memphis, founded by the Menes/Hor-Aha:

> The river used to flow along the base of the sandy hills on the Libyan border, and this monarch [Men], by damming it up at the bend about a hundred furlongs south of Memphis, drained the original channel and diverted it to a new one half-way between the two lines of hills. To this day the elbow which the Nile forms here, where it is forced into its new channel, is most careful watched by the Persians, who strengthen the dam every year; for should the river burst it, Memphis might be completely overwhelmed. On the land which had been drained by the diversion of the river, king Men built the city which is now called Memphis – it lies in the narrow part of Egypt – and afterwards on the north and west sides of the town excavated a lake, communicating with the river, which itself protects it on the east.[7]

As it was built on reclaimed land, Memphis was constantly threatened by the Nile and this was incorporated into its development – as the Nile migrated eastwards the river-front houses gradually were situated further inland. More houses were built along the river front resulting in the wandering of the city boundaries. Therefore, Memphis was not a single location but rather an area which separated the Delta from the main Nile.[8] Today the Nile is some 4km from Memphis due to a course change, although the original river wall has been located inland. Each year the inhabitants of Memphis watched the approaching inundation with trepidation, as a good flood of approximately 8m deep would not affect the town, but should it reach 10m or more, the results would be disastrous. As such, to counter-act this, the enclosure walls surrounding Memphis stood 11–12m high,[9] giving the city the name 'White Walls' (*Ineb Hedj*).

Its favourable position at the base of the Delta helped to control Nile traf-fic and trade, which was distributed throughout Egypt.[10] Memphis was the cult centre for the god Ptah, and was the focus of the Memphite theology of creation which names Ptah as the supreme creator who created simply by thinking and expressing his desires, before the mound of creation emerged from the primeval waters of Nun. As Memphis was the administrative and religious capital, the royal cemeteries were in the surrounding regions at Giza, Saqqara, Dahshur, Abusir and Abu-Roash, covering an area of approximately 35km^2. These pyramid fields were complex cemeteries providing a great deal of information about the administra-tive hierarchy, economy and politics of the period.

Excavations at the pyramid fields at Giza have uncovered a settlement and cem-etery of the workmen from the fourth dynasty, housing the people who built the Great Pyramid.[11] The settlement was intended for temporary conscripted workmen, housed in galleried dormitories with mud-brick sleeping platforms,[12] each sleep-ing 40 men.[13] There were 16 of these galleries, which may have had two floors and housed up to 2000 workmen – half the workforce needed to build the Great Pyramid. Adjacent to the dormitories was a communal dining hall, with a series of mud-brick benches embedded with fish bones, showing this was a staple of their diet.[14] There were also a series of self-contained supervisory houses for the overseers.[15]

The workmen's cemetery provides names, titles and family connections of hundreds of workers, from the overseers to the washermen, showing the settle-ment at Giza was diverse and representative of a typical community. This village also provides evidence of a highly organised corvée system. Every year during the inundation, between July and October, when the fields were flooded the farm-ers could not work the land.[16] The king conscripted these farmers to work on the royal monuments, paying and housing them until the flood abated and they returned to their farms. Inscriptions in the tombs at Giza, as well as the pyramids themselves, indicate they were proud to work on the royal monuments: 'We did this with pride in the name of our great king, Khnum-Khufu.'[17]

Whilst working on the pyramid they were fed well with a diet of fish and meat, shipped on a regular basis directly from the royal agricultural land and silos. The period of conscription may have only lasted for one wet season for unskilled labourers or full time for skilled stonemasons, stone-cutters and administrators.[18]

The Nile was essential to the daily work of building the pyramids, for which these men were instrumental too. The question of how large stone blocks were moved without the aid of cranes is one that will be constantly discussed even with enough evidence to answer it. Water played a key role. The tomb of Djhutihotep

(1929–1841 BCE) from el Bersheh depicts a large statue of the tomb owner being transported to its final resting place using a wooden sledge, pulled by hundreds of men. To facilitate the movement, wooden logs were placed under the sledge and water poured onto the ground to lubricate it; as the sledge progressed the logs were moved from the rear to the front. Water was a key feature in the manoeu-vring of large blocks across the land and the Nile was also used for transporting blocks *to* the pyramid fields themselves. At the time of the inundation, the Nile rose to within a few metres of the pyramids at Giza (fig. 18), running along the plateau edge which dictated their location as well as the quarries used:

> When the Nile overflows, the whole country is converted into a sea and the town ... alone remain above water ... At these times water transport is used all over the country instead of merely along the course of the river, and anyone going from Naukrautis to Memphis would pass right by the pyramids.[19]

Recent studies of the Giza region have further investigated the Nile course, and it is thought that there was a lake or canal running from Meidum to Giza, which during the inundation would have greatly facilitated the movement of blocks to these pyramid sites. At Giza itself there are functioning harbours to the east of the Sphinx, a kilometre from the escarpment edge,[20] which were used for the unload-ing of ships and access to the Giza Plateau. Since the Old Kingdom, the Nile in this region has been migrating eastwards and this may have been aided by the quarrying of the stone used for the pyramids as the waste material was dumped in the Nile.[21] By the time of Menkaure the river was no longer flowing close to the Giza Plateau, and this meant that moving blocks was more problematic for him. Instead of using limestone casing blocks on the pyramid from the quarry on the east bank at Giza, he used granite from Aswan and it has been suggested that this may have been easier to transport with the straight Nile run, rather than what was now a more difficult route to the limestone quarries.[22]

The pyramids are useful to track economic high and low points and, some believe, the ratio of the kings' power against that of the nobles. It is generally accepted, for example, that the fourth-dynasty king Sneferu ruled an economi-cally powerful Egypt as he was able to construct at least three (possibly as many as seven) pyramids at Meidum and Dahshur, using more worked stone than any other king in the Old Kingdom. The real economic high point, however, was the reign of Khufu (2589–2566 BCE) and the construction of the Great Pyramid, although it is often his excesses that are blamed for the economic downturn that followed. By the reign of Unas of the fifth dynasty and Tety of the sixth dynasty, the economy and royal power had diminished, which is reflected in the shoddy pyramid construction of this age, where they are nothing more than piles of rubble with smooth exteriors, which over the years were removed for reuse. The tombs of fifth- and sixth-dynasty princes at Saqqara also show a decline in royal power as they are identical in size to tombs of officials.

The pyramids also reflect a high point in the religious development of the Old Kingdom, following ideas of the pre-dynastic and early dynastic periods when deities focused on the role of the local chieftain in the form of divine power, strength and fertility. The deities worshipped in the Old Kingdom temples were all associated with kingship ideology, and through the worship of the god the divinity of the king was maintained. The Osiris and Seth mythology was fundamental to the ideology of kingship, funerary beliefs and agricultural cycle, as it clarified the laws of succession, enabling the reigning king to trace his ancestry back to creation. The succession became such an important aspect of kingship that, during the twelfth dynasty, the king took a co-regent as a means of identifying his successor before his death to prevent any doubt or potential usurpation.

8 The Giza Pyramids in inundation. (*Reproduced with permission of the Griffith Institute, University of Oxford*)

Through the Osiris and Seth mythology, the king was also associated with Ra and Horus, although some view the increasing popularity of the solar god Ra during the fifth dynasty as a sign of the diminishing power of the king, which was being transferred to the priests of the cult. However, others argue that the rise in the solar cult, particularly in connection with royalty, only further emphasised the divinity of the king in both life (as Ra) and in death (as Osiris). Throughout the Old Kingdom it is possible to trace the rise of the solar cult from the reign of Djoser (2668–2649 BCE), the first king to dedicate a shrine to the solar god at Heliopolis. The solar cult continued to develop until the son of Khufu, Djedefra (2566–2558 BCE), incorporated the name 'Ra' into his own, using the title 'Son of Ra' for the first time.[23] This became part of the standard five-fold titulary until the end of the pharaonic period. The succeeding kings also incorporated Ra into their names (e.g. Khafra, Menkaura) and the first seven kings of the fifth dynasty dedicated temples to the sun god.[24] Ra became the closest thing to a state god and was associated not only with kingship but also the funerary cult, as his nocturnal journey represented that between death and rebirth. These are recorded in the Pyramid Texts, although the ideas may be much older. They initially applied only to the afterlife of the king but by the end of the Old Kingdom some chapters were used in non-royal burials. Different fates were recorded for the king, indicative of various origins of the ideas presented. Utterance 461, for example, describes the king becoming a star, ruling from the sky:

> O King, may you ascend as the morning star, may you be rowed as the lake dweller … may you travel by boat to the Field of Rushes, that you may cultivate barley, that you may reap emmer and prepare your sustenance therefrom like Horus the son of Atum.[25]

It is clear from this spell that the environment and the Nile were great influences, and travelling by boat was a means of travel worthy of the gods, which is further emphasised when the king joins Ra in his solar barque to traverse the night sky until he is reborn in the morning.[26]

After the fourth dynasty, solar symbols were incorporated into the construction of the pyramids, with the entrance on the east facing the land of the living. The top of all pyramids were capped with a Benben stone or pyramidian, a small pyramid-shaped block covered in gold, silver, electrum or copper which is closely associated with the sun and creation, as the shape represents the primeval mound of creation, symbolic of fertility, rebirth and the sun.[27] The *benben* was thought to absorb the first rays of the sun at dawn, channelling them to the earth and creating a join between the earth and sky.[28]

The Egyptian understanding of the environment is also reflected in their manipulation of it. For the crops to be successful each year, forward planning was essential to ensure suitable crops were planted at the right time.[29] During times of famine, if records were well kept of the heights of the Nile floods, they could plan ahead, importing surplus goods for the time when they needed it most, as well as increasing the agricultural land itself through the construction of irrigation canals in times of high floods.[30] All of which would have been carried out locally, under the control of the mayor, although much of the farmland was owned by the king or the newly established temples. Most of the land was farmed using the corvée system, and it is recorded that those who did not meet their conscription obligations were punished and sent to government farms or labour camps. The distribution of work was centrally organised at the 'Office of Assigning People',[31] although how this was organised is not known.

In the early dynastic period, a means for measuring field boundaries was introduced and this was improved throughout the Old Kingdom as a way of not only demarcating temple and royal lands but also the boundaries of Egypt. These borders were set by the environment, with the eastern and western margins marked by a mountain range, and the southern by the Nile cataracts, the oldest features on the Nile.[32] The northern borders were protected by the Mediterranean and, to the north-east, by the Lake of Horus, which rendered only one place of entry from the Sinai. The north-western edge was not as easily defended once the enemy bypassed the western mountains, but they were all protected by local recruits conscripted for duty. Fortified cities existed from the Naqada III period, and it is likely that these were extended to act as fortresses on the Egyptian borders.

As the Old Kingdom progressed, the need to control the flow of immigrants into Egypt arose, leading to the establishment of fortresses by the Middle Kingdom. Along the eastern borders of the Delta, Amenemhat I began the construction of a string of well-defended fortresses which were maintained at least until the reign of Rameses II. The fortresses were situated in such a way as to utilise the natural topography of the region, preventing invasion along the coastal route from the Levant, known as the 'Way of Horus'. Amenemhat I also constructed a fortress in the Wadi Natrun to defend the western borders from the Libyans. The most elaborate fortifications, however, were in the south, indicating that there was a bigger threat from the Nubians than from the east or west. The southern border was marked by the island of Elephantine and the first Nile cataract. In addition to these natural defences, in the twelfth dynasty the border was protected by a huge mud-brick wall, measuring some 7.5km (4.5 miles) long. Due to a great deal of military expansion during the Middle Kingdom, a chain of fortresses was constructed between the first and the second cataracts, and along the land route to the second cataract, in the region of Semna. These fortresses were elaborate, fortified cities, located at the most vulnerable points along the trade route between Egypt and Nubia, acting both as military outposts and customs stations.

Of the 17 fortresses, 11 were clustered in the area of the second cataract, each positioned to control the flow of traffic northwards at points where the Nile was difficult to navigate, forcing people to take the heavily defended land route. Sadly, all of these fortresses were flooded when the Aswan High Dam was constructed.

The Egyptians, however, were not only trading with Nubia, but also with Palestine and the Levant. By the first dynasty the Egyptians were making large-scale, frequent sojourns into the area, perhaps in attempt of colonisation. During the Middle Kingdom there were so many expeditions to the Sinai, particularly for the stone and mineral quarries, that a small shrine dedicated to Hathor, Lady of Turquoise, was built at Serabit el-Khadim, protecting Egyptians in the area.

The Palermo stone records a trading exhibition where 40 ships were used to import wood, possibly from Byblos, during the reign of Sneferu (2613–2589 BCE),[33] who also travelled to Nubia for cattle, raw materials and wood. During the reign of Sahura of the fifth dynasty (2491–2477 BCE), 80,000 units of myrrh and electrum from Punt were imported. No one knows exactly where Punt was, although it is generally accepted to be situated on the Sudan-Eritrea border, reached from Egypt via the Red Sea. There is reference to expeditions to Punt along the route from Koptos to the Red Sea harbour of Wadi Gasus.

Most of the trade was carried out by river where possible, especially during the summer months during the inundation, but once the waters subsided sandbanks emerged which damaged the boats.[34] The cataract area of the Nile was particularly treacherous and slipways were created enabling traders to get past, as well as unsuccessful attempts to deepen the Nile there.[35] The boats were unloaded and placed on the slipway on the river banks, situated near the fortresses which were well placed to defend the boats at their most vulnerable.[36] With good winds, a laden boat sailing against the current could travel a distance of 40km a day, so travelling to the Lebanon (about 500km) could take eight days to get there and 10 days to return.[37] For local day-to-day travel the donkey was the prime mode of transport (fig. 19), as it could carry 100–200kg for up to 20km a day, meaning they were ideal for the transportation of foodstuffs and commodities – a train of 7–14 donkeys was capable of providing a month's supply of food.[38]

Although the Nile still had a very practical use, with the establishment of the hierarchical elite some traditional riverine activities were adopted as pleasurable pastimes, which further separated and defined the classes. Boating was adopted as a competitive sport amongst the elite and fishermen. 'Fishermen's jousting' was depicted in numerous tombs of the Old Kingdom, remaining popular until the New Kingdom, where the objective was to knock each other off their boats with poles (fig. 20). What may have started as harmless fun soon developed into a serious sport with three or four teams participating. One scene, however, depicts the danger as one fisherman lost the contest and fell into the Nile, only to be seized by a crocodile.[39] Despite their threat, crocodiles were not hunted after the end of the early dynastic period, although ritualistically Horus, and therefore the king, were depicted in the process of hunting crocodiles, who when slain represented the god of chaos, Seth, demonstrating the king's power to maintain order. The hippopotamus, on the other hand, was bigger and more dangerous than the crocodile, and was freely hunted by groups of men, watched by the elite.

Left: 19 Donkeys were the most common form of transport

Below: 20 Boat jousting from the tomb of Iymery. Giza

Fishing and fowling were both activities essential for the economy, but by the Old Kingdom this was a ritual act of the king, and the fifth-dynasty funerary temples show Userkaf and Sahura performing this ritual. The elite also went fishing and fowling but for purely recreational purposes in the marshes of the Nile, depicted on private tombs from the Old Kingdom through to the New Kingdom (fig. 21). These images are clearly ritualistic as the inappropriate clothing indicates: the tomb owners are often shown with false beards and royal-style kilts.

The scenes are two-fold, with one half of the composition showing the tomb owner on a papyrus skiff, accompanied by his family and harpooning two fish (a large *lates* and a *tilapia* or two). The *lates* was primarily found in Upper Egypt and the *tilapia* in Lower Egypt,[40] representing a united Egypt. The *tilapia* was associated with rebirth and the god Atum, and is often depicted with a lotus flower, the symbol of creation.[41] The *lates* fish was associated with the goddess Neith, who was believed to have turned herself into this fish to navigate the primordial waters of Nun.

21 Nebamun hunting in the marshes (eighteenth dynasty). British Museum

The other half of the composition shows the tomb owner and his family on the papyrus skiff, catching birds using throwing sticks shaped like boomerangs. The word for 'throw stick' was the same as 'to conceive', accentuating the fertility aspect of these scenes. Although these scenes no doubt represent relaxing family afternoons in the marshes, they are also highly ritualistic. The papyrus skiff is recorded by Plutarch as the method of transportation for Isis when searching for the body of Osiris, and it was believed by the Egyptians that the skiff would not be attacked by crocodiles.[42] This is potentially true as crocodiles are attracted by movement in the water and the skiff produced minimal disturbance. The tomb owner is always shown as young and vibrant, surrounded by his wife and children, showing he is virile and will continue to be so in the afterlife. The methods for capturing the birds and fish were highly ineffectual, but the tomb owner was always successful, displaying not only his strength and skill but that he, like the king and Osiris, was able to tame nature. The *Pleasures of Fishing and Fowling* describes his successes: 'I kill again and again, there being no end for my (harpoon) shaft. I shall fill bags with white Nile perch.'

It is, however, made clear that this is for fun and not practical purposes: 'The gutting of fish is not agreeable to me.' The pleasure was clearly in the hunt itself. The narrator of the *Pleasures* clearly enjoys these days hunting and wishes he could spend every day in such pursuits – a possibility for the rich elite members of society.

Although the Nile now had a frivolous side, it was still central to Egypt's survival and some have suggested it led to the collapse of the Old Kingdom. The Palermo Stone records the Nile floods from the pre-dynastic period to end of the fifth dynasty, taken at the Nilometer at Memphis, known as the 'House of Inundation'.

A period of low Nile struck during the reign of Pepy II (2278–2184 BCE) resulting in failed crops and famine,[43] and indeed the collapse of the Old Kingdom and the Middle Kingdom were heralded by such climatic changes,[44] demonstrating how closely Egyptian civilisation is tied in with the environment. The figures are supported by sediment studies showing that between 2250–2050 BCE there was a period of low floods in the Delta, and evidence from Memphis and Dakhla Oasis indicates that desert sand began to encroach on the towns. Some parts of the river bed were now permanently exposed by the receding waters.

The situation was not aided by the hereditary nature of the positions of power, where the corrupt families now kept more of the crops for themselves, leading to the failure of the centralised administrative system. A constant need for surplus food to feed non-food producers caused conflict between the farmers and the elite, which led to the collapse of the royal court. Locally, nomarchs were still controlling irrigation within their towns, but with no powerful centralised government this also broke down as revenues from these provinces slowly diminished. As the famine got worse farmers died, decreasing the size of the workforce and affecting agricultural activity. As people began to starve, the looting and the destruction of temples and tombs started. This is described in the *Admonitions of Ipuwer*. Although there is some doubt of the actual date of the text, it is generally accepted that this records the chaos of the First Intermediate Period.

> Lo, the private council chamber its writings are stolen,
> Lo offices are opened, Lo their records stolen,
> Lo, scribes are slain, their writings stolen[45]

Before long rioting started and civilisation collapsed, resulting in the king having neither the power nor wealth to hire an army to deal with the situation:

> The grain of Egypt is common property 'I-go-get-it'
> And the palace is without its revenues.
> The king's storehouse is 'I go-get-it' for everyone[46]

This famine was not to last long and the Nile floods stabilised in the Middle Kingdom, leading to an economically stronger Egypt until the death of Amenemhat III; further low Niles saw the collapse of the Middle Kingdom, which led to the Second Intermediate Period, showing a cycle of destruction and rejuvenation.[47] However, none of these economically low and environmentally unstable time periods had any real lasting effects on culture, and Egypt always recovered in a stronger position. Nonetheless, the environmental effects of an increasingly arid climate led to a decline in desert fauna, causing the lament 'the desert is dying of hunger' during the reign of Amenemhat III. Even depictions in temple and tomb images show desert fauna changing over time. The Egyptians simply adapted well to the changing climate and eco-system, developing as a community.

🐂 5 🐂

THE FLOOD AS LAND TO MY FEET

1570–1070 BCE

The economic, political and cultural high point of the pharaonic period was the New Kingdom and, due to royal annals, personal letters, accounts and literary tales, we are able to produce a detailed overview of life during this time. Combined with archaeological excavations, we can add to this knowledge with information regarding the landscape and climate of the period. Egypt as we know it today is very different to that of the New Kingdom, which consisted of many lakes and canals that have since dried up. It is common knowledge that the Nile at Memphis has migrated eastwards in the last few thousand years but at Luxor the river is also migrating westwards.[1]

Excavations at Karnak have shown its construction was greatly influenced by the waterscape, which is changing at a rate of 250m per 1000 years.[2] From the Middle Kingdom there was a water source north of the treasury of Tuthmosis I,[3] and the land between the fifth and sixth pylons was created by Nile dumps, where water had once flowed. The land north and west of Karnak was naturally extended, enabling the constructions of Tuthmosis III and Amenhotep II.[4] It is even suggested that Karnak may once have been built on an island[5] and the series of quays and harbours show where the water was at the time of construction.[6] This tied in well with their ideology, by building their temple upon a mound surrounded by water, indicative of the primordial mound of creation. Photographs taken in 1930 show that since the Napoleonic campaign two islands in front of Luxor and Karnak had joined to the mainland[7] and there are New Kingdom texts that refer to 'new land' or 'islands',[8] indicating they were familiar and accepting of their changing landscape. These islands may have been seen as something sacred, as they would appear from the swirling waters of the Nile and would soon merge with the mainland again. From the time of Akhenaten (1350–1334 BCE) the island of Karnak had started to join to the mainland, and the newly silted areas were built upon. The first pylon at Karnak was directly on the river in the Ptolemaic period and excavations have uncovered Ptolemaic baths in front of the pylon, behind the Sphinx Avenue which would have sat by the river. By the Roman period, Karnak was no longer an island,[9] although an artificial canal had been kept connecting the main temple with the Temple of Montu.[10]

This changing landscape was a result of the variable Nile floods as well as an increase in New Kingdom flash floods. Throughout the reign of Merenptah (1212–1202 BCE) until the end of the Ramesside period, there are continuing references to flash floods, caused by localised bursts of rain: 'On this day, coming down of the water in the sky.'[11]

For most of the year Egypt suffered from northerly winds originating in the monsoonal lows of India, and spring and autumn were generally times of climate change, causing winds and heavy rainfall on the eastern mountains. Such weather was also recorded: 'Regnal year 52, month 3 of *peret*, day 3, the wind being from the south, strong.'[12]

The resulting rainfall caused flash floods in the wadis during October and November. As the clouds moved towards the river, the air mass became unstable creating cumulonimbus (thunderstorm) clouds gravitating towards the cliffs surrounding the Valley of the Kings.[13] Each cloud could hold half a million tons of water which fell in localised regions, making them difficult to predict and therefore manage. Through studies of the Valley of the Kings over the last few decades the paths of these flash floods have been identified. Seven streams in the Valley existed: one directed at KV55 and another at KV62.[14] Three streams met in the central area, creating a mass of turbulent water which was channelled out of the Valley.[15] As these three central streams lost velocity, sediment settled over the area concealing any tomb entrances. Currently, natural bedrock lies 5m below the current path, showing the depth of sedimentation over the centuries. In March 2009 a manmade drainage channel was discovered close to KV8 in the cliffs, between the tombs of Ramesses II and Merenptah, possibly dug to divert water away from the tombs. This water, pooled in a sacred basin at the bottom of the cliffs, and an ostracon discovered here mentions a sacred tree growing here where 'tears of the gods' were collected. The inundation was believed to be caused by a single tear falling into the river from the eye of Isis as she mourned her dead husband, Osiris,[16] and it is easy to see the connection in the minds of the Egyptians between the inundation and these localised flash floods.

The flood layers over the tomb entrances enable us to pinpoint exactly when such floods occurred; for example, over the entrance of Tutankhamun's tomb (KV62), the flood layer is 0.9m thick, and 1.2m deep over the entrance to KV55, which sits lower in the valley floor, suggesting there was a flash flood not long after the death of Tutankhamun that concealed both tombs. The increase in flash floods was also considered when constructing the royal tombs, and those built after Thutmosis III had a well shaft known as the 'Hall of Waiting' or 'Hall of Hindrance', which had two purposes: one, to protect the burial chamber from flash floods, and, two, to act as a deterrent to tomb robbers. However, as time passed these shafts obtained religious significance as the burial place of the mortuary god Sokar.[17] Even after the reign of Ramses III, when the well was no longer excavated, the room was still included in the construction, showing its practical element was forgotten but the ritualistic one was not.

Whereas the flash floods needed to be controlled to limit damage to tombs, houses and livestock, records do not indicate how or if this water was utilised in the same way as the inundation was. Records show that dykes and dams were used to guide water during the inundation[18] but the unpredictability of the flash floods may have rendered this impossible. The Egyptians made good use of the annual flood waters for agriculture, pleasure lakes and transportation, through the use of irrigation canals, channelling the water where it was needed most. In order to increase the amount of agricultural land available, in the New Kingdom the *shaduf* was introduced (fig. 22). This water-moving device comprised a long wooden handle with a bucket on one end and a weight on the other, and when the bucket was full it was swung around and emptied into an irrigation canal on higher ground. Each *shaduf* could lift water a height of 3m, so when used in tandem could raise water to much higher levels.[19] These are still used in rural areas of Egypt even today.

The Nile floods were also manipulated to fill pleasure lakes, pools and baths, as the recreational use of the river was further developed (plate 4). The largest pleasure lake was that of Amenhotep III at Malkata, south of Luxor, constructed for his wife Tiye in year 11. The excavation of the lake was recorded on no less than 11 ceremonial scarabs:

> His Majesty commanded the making of a lake for the great royal wife Tiy, may she live, in her town Djarukha. Its length is 3700 (cubits) and its width is 700 (cubits). (His Majesty) celebrated the festival of opening the lake in the third month of inundation, day 16. His Majesty was rowed in the royal barge Aten-tjehen in it.[20]

The T-shaped lake was 2km long by 1km wide, and the earth removed during the excavation of the lake created an artificial platform upon which the palace and Amenhotep III's mortuary temple were built. The remainder was heaped into rows of small mounds, which are still visible 4500 years later (fig. 23). An inscription from the tomb of Kheruef describes how the lake was used during the *sed* festival of Amenhotep, to carry the divine statues on the king's morning

22 Shaduf in action (nineteenth century). (*Courtesy of Photos.com*)

and evening barques, and towed to the steps of the palace, in imitation of the journey of the sun god through the day and night skies.[21] The lake was filled via a canal from the Nile, meaning the lake contained fish which the king could catch (fig. 24). The royal barge *The Dazzling Aten*, used by the royal couple for their religious and royal festivals as well as pleasure trips on this lake, was moored in the harbour attached.

Although the Nile was a great source of pleasure, it was a place of danger housing large predators such as crocodiles and hippopotamuses. From the first dynasty reign of Den, hippopotamus hunting took place[22] as an incarnation of Seth and an element of the ideologies of kingship. Crocodiles are, on the other hand, considered a more realistic danger to the ordinary people and the Middle Kingdom Satire of the Trades states:

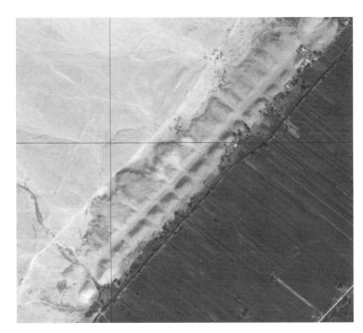

Left: 23 The mounds of earth at Malkata. (© *2009 Google Earth*)

Below: 24 New Kingdom official fishing in his garden

The washerman launders at the riverbank in the vicinity of the crocodile. I shall go away, father, from the flowing water, said his son and his daughter, to a more satisfactory profession, one more distinguished than any other profession.

I mention for you also the fisherman. He is more miserable than one of any other profession, one who is at his work in a river infested with crocodiles. When the totalling of his account is made for him, then he will lament. One did not tell him that a crocodile was standing there, and fear has now blinded him.[23]

Although crocodile hunting was not popular, or at least not recorded, they were clearly feared. The crocodile god Sobek was worshipped in Upper Egypt to appease the god so he would remove the danger of crocodiles from the Nile (fig. 25).

25 Sobek and Amenhotep III. Luxor Museum

However, it was the smaller creatures living in and around the Nile that proved fatal to the communities living there. The most common disease in both ancient and modern Egypt was bilharzia, (Schistosomiasis) a parasitic worm released by the water snail which penetrates the skin and enters the veins. These water snails live in stagnant water, and during the inundation, when most of the land was covered, people were unable to avoid walking through knee-deep water. Bilharzia causes anaemia, loss of appetite, urinary infection and deterioration of the immune system.

Water supplies were easily infected with other worms if close to latrines[24] or other sources of stagnant water. One mummy from the Manchester Museum shows the remains of the Guinea worm in the abdominal wall, contracted through drinking water containing immature forms of the worm. Another mummy called Natsefamun, also from Manchester Museum, worked closely with the sacred bulls at Karnak. One of his most interesting parasitic worms was the filarial worm which causes elephantiasis. Two species of mosquito carry lymphatic filariasis, one that bites primarily at night and the second breeds in unclean water, drains and cesspools. It could take up to 20 years for the infection from the parasitic worm to develop into fully-fledged elephantiasis, characterised by nodular, warty changes to the thickening skin.[25] These symptoms are difficult to detect in mummies but examination of Natsefamun's scrotum presented evidence of the adult parasitic filaria worm. It is impossible to see at which stage of the disease Natsefamun had reached, although if he had been in the later stages he may have had a grossly enlarged scrotum and swollen legs.

Although the Nile was such a source of danger, it was also used in some medicinal treatments, particularly the silt which was believed to represent great fertility. Fish were also used in medicinal care, and the blood of the *synodontis* was used as an eyelash treatment, while the bile of the *abdu* fish was used to treat the eyes.[26] The dangers of the Nile, however, were simply considered a fact of life, and there was a duality in its appearance being both dangerous and healing. In the New Kingdom love poem recorded on the Cairo Vase, the river is represented as a barrier fraught with danger keeping two lovers apart:

My sister's love is on yonder side,
The river is between our bodies;
The waters are mighty at [flood] time,
A crocodile waits in the shallows.
I enter the water and brave the waves,
My heart is strong on the deep;
The crocodile seems like a mouse to me.
The flood as land to my feet.
It is her love that gives me strength,

It makes a water-spell for me;
I gaze at my heart's desire,
As she stands facing me.[27]

In another love poem, recorded on Papyrus Harris, the river is described as being a sacred entity, the livelihood of the narrator and his means of transportation to the temple of Ptah at Memphis:

I fare north in the ferry by the oarsman's stoke,
On my shoulder my bundle of reads;
I am going to Memphis to tell Ptah, Lord of Truth
Give me my sister tonight!
The river is as if of wine, its rushes are Ptah,
Sekhmet is its foliage, Iadet its buds
Nefertem its lotus blossoms

These two poems emphasise the duality of the river in the minds of the Egyptians: something ordinary, whose dangers can be overcome as well as something sacred to be revered. This belief in the divinity of the river led to its inclusion in religion, both in the processions and rituals.

Water and the Nile feature heavily in the mythology surrounding the major deities of the pantheon. It appears in the creation myths in the form of Nun, the primordial lake from which all creation started, as well as being essential in the funerary mythology surrounding Osiris, as he was drowned when he was cast into the river within an elaborately carved chest by his brother Seth. Even in the *Contendings of Horus and Seth*, Horus devised a competition for the throne of Egypt involving a Nile race in stone ships. The entire nocturnal journey of the sun god, upon his solar barque, takes place on water reminiscent of the Nile, and indeed the landscape of the underworld resembles Egypt at its best. With such a prominent element of the religious ideology it is hardly surprising to see the Nile featuring heavily in religious ceremonies.

Every temple in Egypt had an element of the primeval waters of Nun, in the form of the sacred lake which was dug down to sub-soil water, ensuring a self-feeding supply (plate 5).[28] These lakes were accessed by a staircase for purification rituals of the priests before entering the temple and were also used for re-enactments of sacred mythology, such as sailing the sacred barques (fig. 26),[29] and to supply water for the rituals within the temple.[30] The lake at Karnak was also able to recreate the time of creation, with small tunnels attached to geese pens through which a goose was pushed. It miraculously appeared upon the water, as if from nowhere[31] and, as a symbol of Amun, was taken as a good omen.[32]

26 Sacred barque of Mutemwia.
British Museum

The Nile was used as an extension of these sacred lakes in most religious festivals. The most important national festival was the New Year's festival or the
Festival of the Nile, celebrated on the first day of the inundation and considered
a time of rejuvenation and rebirth. Prayers were offered to Hapy, the god of the
inundation, to prevent the flood being too high or low, both of which resulted in
famine, death and disease. It was celebrated with a procession through the streets
where statues of Hapy were carried upon the shoulders of priests so they could
be addressed by the worshippers.[33] This festival was celebrated with great aplomb
at the city on Elephantine in particular, considered to be the source of the Nile.

Although the New Year festival was important, in Thebes there were two major
festivals, the Festival of Opet and the Beautiful Festival of the Valley, both featuring
the Nile. The Festival of Opet was set by the lunar calendar and was held in the
second month of the year (15 July–15 August), not long after the New Year festivities. Although the majority of records of this festival date to the New Kingdom, it
may be much older (fig. 27). The festival celebrated the divinity, virility and fertility
of the king, his association with and protection by the god Amun. The main event
in this festival was a procession between Karnak and Luxor temples, where the
statue of Amun was carried in his barque by priests. The procession to Luxor was
accompanied by musicians, dancers and a military parade along the Sphinx Avenue,
led by the king. The god stayed at Luxor temple, his 'southern harem', for 20 days

before the procession back to Karnak, along the river. The riverine procession was led by the royal barge, enabling the people lining the banks to see the king and the divine boat carrying the statue of Amun towed by smaller boats. The boats were painted in bright colours and fragments of funerary boats from Dashur have retained these colours; hulls were painted green with a thin black line and thicker red lines decorating the gunwales. The oars were decorated with wadjet eyes, lotus flowers and coloured bands. For 11 days after the procession back to Karnak, the local community celebrated with beer and food provided by the temple.

The Beautiful Festival of the Valley was associated with rebirth and the dead. It was held in the tenth month of the year (15 March–15 April) and, although prominent in the New Kingdom, can be traced to the Middle Kingdom. The procession started at Karnak temple, where the statue of Amun was placed in a shrine atop his sacred barque. Ramses II records that the priests carrying the divine barques wore masks of hawk and jackal heads representing the primordial spirits of the ancient religious centres of Upper and Lower Egypt – perhaps the 'Followers of Horus', as discussed in Chapter 3. This procession, like the others, was greeted by the local population, who wanted to get close to an otherwise inaccessible god. The statue was carried to the quay at Karnak, to be joined by statues of his wife Mut and their child Khonsu. The three divine barques were placed onto the *Userhet*, a 67ft-long barge covered with gold and precious materials, built from imported Lebanese cedar and transported to the west bank.

27 Opet Festival, Karnak

A flotilla of smaller boats followed the royal barge, towing the divine barque across the Nile to the mortuary temples. This procession was accompanied by acrobats, musicians and the general population, and ended in the necropolis to visit the royal mortuary temples. The people separated as they approached the tombs of their ancestors, where they left offerings of food and drink within the mortuary chapels and 'feasted' with them. They then spent the night sleeping in the funerary chapels, hoping their ancestors might communicate with them through their dreams. Although this festival in its entirety was annual, the ancestors and the deceased divine kings were not neglected – every 10 days the statue of Amun-Re of Luxor visited the tomb of the primordial gods on the west bank.

The Nile was the quickest and easiest way of transporting a lot of people from one place to another, whether for ceremonial or practical purposes, and was used in the New Kingdom for the extensive temple building projects and the transportation of large blocks of stone from the quarries of Nubia and Giza. An image on the causeway of Unas shows the transportation of two large stone columns, indicating transportation of heavy objects by river was not a New Kingdom innovation, although there was an increase in heavy river traffic during this time. One of the most impressive recorded transportation feats was carried out during the reign of Hatshepsut in year 16 (1488 BCE), recorded at her mortuary temple at Deir el Bahri. She commissioned two obelisks, quarried from red granite in Aswan, together weighing over 1000 tonnes, which were transported to Thebes using low rafts of 100m long by 30m wide. They were too cumbersome to sail so were towed by smaller vessels using the flow of the current[34] or the waters of the inundation.[35] Due to the size of the barges, it is unlikely they could be towed against the tide, so if they were to be reused they would be dismantled in Thebes and reassembled in Aswan. The obelisks themselves have long since disappeared so the exact heights are unknown, but they were erected at Karnak amidst a public festival of celebration. It took seven months from the start of construction to completion.[36] Of the four obelisks Hatshepsut erected at Karnak only one still stands and is the tallest in Egypt at 29.5m (96ft 9in),[37] weighing 323 tons.

Hatshepsut also records at Deir el Bahri an expedition to Punt, which, from the flora and fauna depicted, was probably situated in Africa, perhaps Ethiopia or Eritrea,[38] although some scholars suggest Somalia, Djibouti or even Zanzibar.[39] The inscriptions make it clear it was reached via the Red Sea[40] and was a source of ivory, wood, gold, apes, exotic animals, frankincense and myrrh trees. These trees were brought to Egypt, roots included, and planted alongside the causeway leading to her temple. The tree pits can still be seen today. The expedition to Punt was a large one and was accompanied by at least five shiploads of soldiers,[41] showing that there was an effective navy in existence despite the early stage of the army's existence. Soldiers were employed for these journeys for their strength when quarrying or loading the ships, as well as for their military training, protecting the expedition on the journey there and back. As Punt was reached via the Red Sea, the ships sailed north from Thebes to Koptos, where they were unloaded and dismantled. These were then carried across the eastern desert to Quesir on the Red Sea, where they were reconstructed before continuing on the sea-borne part of the voyage. Some vessels may have been dragged along the desert in one piece and excavations of twelfth-dynasty boats at Dashur show a wooden sledge was used for their transportation across the desert.[42] It is thought these boats were probably not dismantled for the return journey but rather left at the Red Sea to save on the complex job of returning to the Nile with the boats.[43]

Due to the importance of the Nile as a mode of transport, various port sites were situated along the river at Elephantine, Thebes, Koptos, Memphis and Avaris/Pi-Ramesses, although there may have been a series of quays used for unloading at various points along the river.[44] The port at Elephantine was built to deal with the increasing quarrying of granite in Nubia, although there was a settlement here from the Naqada II to the medieval period.[45] In the north, Memphis was the main port during the Old Kingdom, maintaining this role throughout the New Kingdom. The texts describe Memphis as the 'Great shipyard of the palace' and 'dockyard on the island of Ptah', indicating that the port was a key feature of the city. At present the Nile is at least 3km from Memphis, but during the New Kingdom the city was adjacent to the Nile as the river has migrated eastwards over the centuries.[46] During the early New Kingdom, Peru-nefer was a large port which was particularly important as a starting point for the military and stopping point for merchants, and is believed by some to be the Memphite port. The name Peru-nefer means the 'good going forth' or the 'good exit', and was the starting point of long journeys.[47] A stela of Amenhotep II states he travelled from Peru-nefer to Memphis,[48] indicating they were different places, which has led some scholars to state that Peru-nefer was at Tell el Dab'a/Qantir. Although the majority of the textual references to Peru-nefer are from Memphis, there is no archaeological evidence to support such a large harbour here.[49] There are, however, signs of at least two large harbours at Pi-Ramesses (Qantir). One of which runs parallel to a fortification wall built by Horemheb (1321–1293 BCE), covering a private access canal and an outlet leading to the Nile which could house hundreds of ships. The second was beside a Hyksos palace built using a defunct Nile channel which created a seasonal lake during the inundation. The Kamose stela, recording the expulsion of the Hyksos, records destroying hundreds of ships at Avaris and either harbour could have housed these.

The site of Ramses II's capital city, Pi-Ramesses, was identified in the 1970s in the modern region of Khata'ana-Qantir/Tell el Dab'a, with continuous settlement from the Middle Kingdom. There were two mounds at the site, one bearing the Hyksos capital Avaris (Tell el Dab'a) and the other Pi-Ramesses (Qantir), with a natural gateway between them blocking the entrance to the Delta, whilst providing large, easily-controlled harbours for shipping and trade.[50] Khata'ana-Qantir was chosen as it was accessible by both road and water – a waterway from Sile called the 'Lake of Horus' and the military 'Horus Road', a busy route leading to the Sinai, Palestine, and the Mediterranean.[51]

Pi-Ramesses was used as the staging post for the troops of Ramses II when marching to Kadesh in year 5 and there is a great military presence at the site. The royal military stables in the city housed up to 460 horses, including military and royal horses. This building was also used for the production of chariots and horse tack. Recent excavations have also uncovered a workshop producing Hittite shields, indicating that there were Hittite mercenaries in the Egyptian army living at Pi-Ramesses. The ongoing excavations at Qantir have uncovered the remains of palaces, houses, royal workshops, temples and numerous statues,[52] and it was recorded that Pi-Ramesses was thought to rival the beauty and splendour of Thebes. The scribe Pabesa in Papyrus Anastasi III records:

> It is a fair spot, there is not the like of it: resembling Thebes, it was Ra who founded it himself. The Residence is agreeable to live in, its fields are full of all good things; it is furnished with abundant provision everyday: its backwaters are full of fishes and its pools of birds, it meadows are verdant with herbage, the greenery is a cubit and half in height. Its granaries are full of wheat and spelt they draw near to the sky … pomegranates, apples and olives: figs from the orchard; sweet wine of Kenkaure surpassing honey, red rw-fish from the lake of the residence … the Lakes of Horus yield salt and *phr*-natron. Its ships fare forth and return to port.[53]

Water was clearly an important factor of the landscape of Pi-Ramesses, and this found its way into the homes and palaces of the people who lived there. In one of the palaces, the dining room or women's quarters was decorated with faience tiles depicting marsh scenes, complete with aquatic plants, fish and swimming girls. In close proximity to one of the palaces was a limestone basin (3m square), with four steps on each side, which was probably used as a bath, filled by a roofed aqueduct nearby. The surrounding area was paved in limestone[54] and it is thought it may have been open to the sky. A similar structure was found amongst the houses of the palace officials, suggesting it was not just a royal luxury. The late Hyksos and early eighteenth-dynasty palaces at the site of Avaris had clean running water as the discovery of a water pipe in the area indicates. This water pipe contains the remains of fish, showing the water was fresh in the pipe.[55] What this water was used for once it reached the palace is not clear but it may have filled pleasure pools and baths or irrigated elaborate gardens. Tell el Dab'a/Qantir was a royal residence from the Middle Kingdom until the end of the twentieth dynasty,[56] and Ramses II spent most of the year here, only travelling to Thebes for official visits and festivals.[57] The city continued to be a bustling metropolis throughout the Ramesside period, when it had expanded covering 4–5km square, including a suburban zone, royal area and foreign colonies, and was still the main defensive frontier of the north.[58] However, when the Pelusaic branch of the Nile silted up in the twentieth dynasty, Pi-Ramesses was abandoned as there was no longer a water supply to the city making habitation impossible. The capital was therefore moved from Pi-Ramesses to Tanis, the only suitable available harbour in the region.[59]

As well as being the site of Ramses II's capital city, the Delta saw the first recorded naval battle in history. When Ramses III (1182–1151 BCE) came to the throne it was a turbulent time, following years of attacks from Libyans during the reign of his predecessor Merenptah. In the early years of Ramses III, the Libyans attacked again with 30,000 men and were able to penetrate the fortresses on the borders of the western Delta. Ramses records killing 12,535 men and taking 1000 prisoner in his victory battle against them. The Libyans lost this battle but returned in year 8, having joined myriad tribes from the coastal areas of Asia Minor and the Aegean, collectively known as the Sea Peoples.

This army, comprising numerous tribes with different skills, was powerful, and were not only skilled at fighting on land but also at sea. On land the Sea Peoples fought in a similar way to the Hittites, with large cumbersome chariots posing little threat to the Egyptians with their lighter and faster chariots. On water, however, their ships were smaller and faster than the Egyptian vessels, and the Egyptians were not comfortable fighting at sea. However, the Sea Peoples were unable to fight and row at the same time, as there were no separate oarsmen. The Egyptian vessels, on the other hand, had 24 oarsmen as well as a contingent of soldiers. The oarsmen were well protected from attack by the high sides of the ships, and these vessels have the earliest recorded crow's nests, used for observation purposes and as a shooting post (fig. 28).

The battle is recorded at Medinet Habu and describes both the land and sea battles. The land battle, led by the king in his chariot, was an easy victory as the Egyptian army was well trained and disciplined. The sea battle was not so simple. The Sea Peoples approached the canals of the Delta using one of the eastern branches of the Nile. The Egyptian fleet, rather than blocking the entry into the canal, followed the Sea Peoples in, blocking their exit. The Egyptians were able to carefully manoeuvre their vessels so as to trap the enemy against the shore which was lined with Egyptian archers. Archers also lined up on the decks of the Egyptian vessels, firing thousands of arrows at the enemy ships. Some were using fire arrows, setting the wooden ships alight. Once the enemy ships were within

28 The first image of a crow's nest. Medinet Habu

range the Egyptians rammed them with the decorative prows of their boats, enabling them to board the ships. Any Sea Peoples jumping overboard and swimming to shore were caught in a volley of arrows from the land-based Egyptians. If they reached the shore they would be captured. There was no escape for the invaders.

Needless to say the battle was a great victory for the Egyptians, who did not rate themselves as great seafaring sailors but clearly showed they were able to guide vessels on the Nile. The battle taking place in the canals of the Delta rather than the Mediterranean would have been familiar territory to the Egyptians, as they were aware of the currents and nature of the river, clearly putting them at an advantage.

At the end of the battle, it was common practice to celebrate with a victory parade on the Nile, sailing the full length of Egypt where captives and booty were transported to their final destination, which, during the New Kingdom, was inevitably the temple of Amun at Karnak. During the reign of Tutankhamun, an image depicts such a victory parade, where a Syrian chief was suspended from the prow of the boat in a cage, showing the strength and power of the king as well as a demonstration of the suppression of foreign enemies and chaos. These parades were as much about celebration at the defeat of the enemy as about kingship ideology, and the divine support the king received from Amun. These processions greatly resembled those of the religious festivals, further showing a combination of the practical and the divine.

The use of the Nile, it can be seen, in the New Kingdom was circular and interconnected, with practical, religious and leisurely uses all having a secondary purpose. Irrigation canals were used to fill pleasure lakes, used for both relaxation and religious ceremonies as well as irrigating the fields for agricultural purposes (fig. 29). The Nile was used for practical transportation of goods and people, as well as the religious and political processions – a worthy highway for both the mundane and divine. The Nile was essential to everyone regardless of their position in life or career, and was utilised in the New Kingdom to its full potential, despite environmental changes and natural disasters which affected not only the Nile, but the flow of day-to-day life.

29 Farmers from the tomb of Nebamun (eighteenth dynasty). British Museum

6

GIFT OF THE NILE

1080–332 BCE

The Third Intermediate and Late Periods were politically complex and appear somewhat chaotic after the relative peace of the New Kingdom. At the collapse of the New Kingdom, Egypt declined politically and economically, resulting in a divided land and continuing invasions from external forces. The dynastic groups of this era can be classified into the Libyan period, the High Priests of Amun, the Nubian period, the Saite Dynasty and the two Persian Periods separated by a time of Egyptian independence. Each period, although some were contemporary with each other, had something to offer the economy and politics of Egypt.

Due to the divided nature of the time, centralised control over farming, irrigation and food production was not possible and these became localised activities. Despite this fragmentation, Herodotus (447 BCE) claimed in his *Histories* that Egypt was 'The gift of the Nile', indicating that the river remained a constant even when the politics and economy were diminished. Due to the fragmentation of the state, Egypt became introverted, concentrating on its own survival and existence,[1] resulting in diminished royal power and neglected contacts with the outside world. Trade with Nubia had collapsed and the *Tale of Wenamun* indicates that Egypt's influence in the Levant had also decreased,[2] to the point that Wenamun was kept waiting and was charged for the goods he had gone to trade, whereas during the New Kingdom goods were handed over as tribute. Their control and influence was at such a low point that, for the first time in Egyptian history, the Egyptian king, Siamun (978–959 BCE) sent his daughter to Solomon of Israel as a diplomatic bride. New Kingdom kings had emphasised that Egyptian queens were never exchanged in marriage, although foreign princesses were sent to Egypt. This gives some idea of Egypt's political standing during the Third Intermediate and Late Periods.

The weakened royal power had a direct impact on the economy as prior to this period there was a centralised storage and distribution network,[3] and as the palace economy collapsed so did the distribution network, meaning villages needed to rely once again on local economy, storage and distribution. The country now lived by hand-to-mouth with small scale exchanges between households and villages for household goods and foodstuff.[4]

This localised storage system relied on the local harvest and basin irrigation, and this in turn was crucially dependant on the annual inundation which varied from year to year. This meant that if a crop failed locally, there was no centralised government to prevent the population from starving. However, this seemed to make the Egyptians more determined to succeed; Herodotus was particularly impressed with the system of dykes employed during the First Persian Period and the ease in which the Egyptians tended the fields, the system of letting the flood waters recede before sowing seeds and using pigs to trample them into the ground. Pigs were also used to help with the threshing during the harvest, eliminating any need for human interaction. This apparent ease had clearly come from centuries of agricultural practice and would vary throughout the country depending on the crops sown and the soil type available.

During this period some areas were richer and more powerful than others, dependant on the amount of land and resources available to the ruling classes. Thebes, in the south, was possibly one of the more powerful divisions, and at the beginning of the period the High Priests of Amun from Karnak had taken over the throne of Upper Egypt, whereas Lower Egypt was ruled by the twenty-first dynasty at Tanis. Herihor, the High Priest of Amun during the reign of Ramses XI, acquired so much power that taking control was easy and he ruled alongside Ramses, who was king in name only. At this time Karnak temple owned two-thirds of all temple land, 90 per cent of all shops and 8 per cent of all factories, mines and ships, putting them in total economic control of Egypt. Herihor, in addition to his priestly titles, held the titles of Vizier and Viceroy of Kush, giving him control of the gold mines of Nubia. Thus it appears that Ramses in his piety had bestowed too many gifts upon the priesthood, making them wealthier than him. Ramses did not have the power or the wealth to oppose him, and upon his death the Theban throne passed to the high priests.

At Tanis, on the other hand, the twenty-first dynasty were of Libyan descent, and Osorkon the Elder (984–978 BCE) was the son of Sheshonq, the chief of the Libyan Meshwesh,[5] who were generally feared by the Egyptians. The Delta, however, was largely ignored by the Egyptians and used primarily for grazing cattle.[6] From the campaigns of Merenptah and Ramses III, Libyans settled here in great numbers, enabling them, like the Hyksos before them, to gain enough local support to take over the throne – made easier by the collapse of the centralised state. Although Tanis was an important site at this time, no remains of a settlement or royal palace have been discovered there, leading some to conclude that they lived at Memphis[7] and used Tanis as a sacred area and burial ground. Their burials were discovered beneath the smaller Mut temple at Tanis in 1939 by Pierre Montet, and included those of Osorkon II, Sheshonq III, Takeloth II and the son of Osorkon, Prince Hornakht, all of the twenty-second dynasty. A couple of weeks later the tombs of Sheshonq II (twenty-second dynasty), Siamun and Pasebkhanut (Psusennes) II (twenty-first dynasty) were also discovered. These burials were constructed beneath the temple complex, allowing the kings to be nearer to the gods. The burial of Psusennes II was the only royal burial ever found intact in Egypt. The mummy, wearing a gold mask (plate 6) and buried in a silver anthropoid coffin (plate 7), was placed within a black granite anthropoid sarcophagus. This in turn lay inside the red granite sarcophagus of Merenptah,[8] which was transported from the Valley of the Kings by river to Tanis. The Tanis burials contained a great deal of gold and silver, demonstrating the wealth of the Tanite dynasty as well as the skill of the metal workers (fig. 30).[9] Silver during the Late Period was used in the market instead of gold, measured in *kite* (9.53g), to be exchanged for services and goods.[10] By the Persian Period silver coins were introduced, some stamped with hieroglyphic and demotic signs, but the value was not specified.[11] Although the monetary system was not fully introduced until Alexander the Great, the Egyptians were familiar with the idea of silver coins a few decades earlier. The lack of gold in the north of Egypt was due to the trade route being difficult between Tanis and Nubia, which was controlled by the High Priests of Amun. It was therefore easier for them to trade silver with the northern and eastern sources.

Although Egypt was divided, they were amicable and the priests of Amun strengthened their relationship with the northern kings through diplomatic marriages, and Sheshonq I (twenty-second dynasty) appointed his son Iupet as High Priest of Amun of Upper Egypt and also appointed supporters of his dynasty and members of the royal house into positions of power in the south[12] in an attempt to reunite Egypt according to tradition. However, this was not to be and the Delta fractured further, with the twenty-second dynasty (945–712 BCE) ruling from Tanis, the twenty-third dynasty (818–712 BCE) ruling from the Central Delta town of Leontopolis and the twenty-fourth dynasty (727–715 BCE) ruling from Sais in the western Delta. Each town was built as a potential rival to Thebes, which further diminished the economy and strength of Egypt. This fractured state was to continue until the Nubian king, Piankhi (twenty-fifth dynasty) invaded Egypt, defeating Osorkon IV (730–1715 BCE)[13] and thereby uniting Egypt.

Before the Nubian conquest, each faction had an active royal policy of building works and primarily defensive military campaigns. Sheshonq I, for example, reopened the Gebel Silsileh quarry in the south, using the stone to build a colonnaded forecourt at Karnak in front of the second pylon. This adoption of the Egyptian religion can also be seen in the burials of the Libyan dynasty, as some of them included a surrounding corridor which flooded, representing the primeval waters from which all life began and the association of deceased with the drowning and rebirth of Osiris.

The Delta landscape was reintroduced and emphasised during this period in the mythology focussing on the childhood of Horus, who after his father's death was raised in the marshes by his mother Isis until he was old enough to take over the throne. Images of Horus the child and Horus *cippi* became popular, which depicts Horus upon the back of a crocodile holding a snake in each hand, showing his dominance over the forces of chaos.

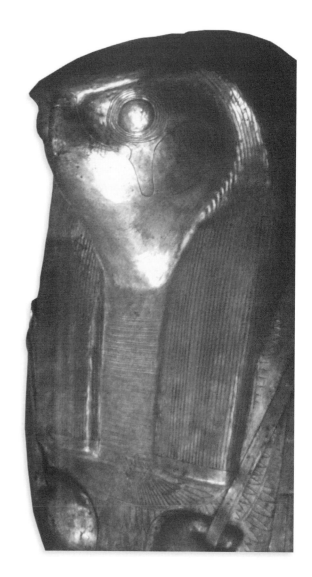

30 Silver hawk headed coffin. Tanis (*The Ancient Egypt Picture Library*)

However, with the decreased international trade, financing huge religious building works and royal burials was difficult. In the south, funding was acquired by
the appropriation of burial goods of the New Kingdom kings from the Valley of
the Kings. The Priests of Amun located the tombs, rewrapped the bodies, removing anything of value before placing the mummies in a cache. Although the kings
in the north did not have such a rich source of gold as the Valley of the Kings,
there was a great importance attached to the reuse of building materials and natural resources,[14] enabling them to maintain Egyptian practices of building to the
gods, foreign expeditions and elaborate burials. Foreign expeditions were also a
great source of wealth for the northern kings, which was unavailable to those in
the south. An inscription of Osorkon from Bubastis mentions statues and utensils
in the temple amounting to 391 tons of gold and silver objects which may have
been obtained during his Palestinian campaign. With no other source of gold or
silver from within Egypt, such campaigns were essential.

The Nubian period was really the start of the end of the pharaonic period,
as they were the first kings to rule remotely from their home country. In 747
BCE Piankhi took over Thebes and proceeded northwards, defeating the Libyan
kings in the Delta and finally uniting Egypt under one king. He ruled Egypt
from Napata in Nubia, although Memphis was chosen as a control point in the
north, where the later king Taharqa (690–664 BCE) was crowned in order to show
that they were upholding Egyptian traditions.[15] During the many centuries of
Egyptian control of Nubia, the Nubians had become Egyptianised and were avid
worshippers of the god Amun (fig. 31).

In order to maintain peace during the reign of Piankhy, Egyptian princes went
to pay their respects to the new king, only to be refused entry on the pretext they
were not circumcised and ate fish, which was considered taboo in the Nubian
palace.[16] Fish was a staple of the Egyptian diet and Herodotus records that everyone in the Delta owned a fishing net and some people lived exclusively on fish.
Plutarch records that priests were the only Egyptians who avoided eating fish due
to its association with the Osiris and Seth mythology, as the fish ate Osiris' penis
when it was thrown into the Nile. In the Late Period fish seem to feature more
often in religious mythology and taboos than in earlier times, although the reason
for this is unclear. For example the *lates* during the Late Period was associated
with Neith, who once turned herself into the fish to explore the depths of the
primeval waters of Nun. Her main cult was at the temple of Esna and mummified
lates were discovered there. It was forbidden to eat the *lates* in the region of Edfu
because of its sacred nature.[17]

Although the Egyptians were refused entry to the palace on this occasion,
Piankhy's successor, Shabaka (716–702 BCE), was not so repelled by the Egyptians
and ruled for 14 years from Memphis, maintaining a good relationship with

the Egyptians and the Assyrians, who were an increasing threat from the East.[18] Shabaka was keen to show his continuation of traditional Egyptian religion and commissioned the Shabaka Stone (fig. 32), which recorded the Memphite theology, naming Ptah as the supreme creator, who did so through the power of thought and word.

The Nubians continued ruling from Memphis until the reign of Taharqa (690–664 BCE). In year 6 of his reign Egypt suffered an abnormally high flood, wiping out the large rat and mice problem which created a larger than usual harvest. His reign therefore became economically strong, which he demonstrated by building extensively throughout Egypt and Nubia. However, an inscription at Karnak mentions in year 15 that dwindling eastern tribute was causing economic problems as many luxury and essential items were imported via this tribute system.[19]

31 Taharqa and Amun. British Museum

32 Shabaka Stone. British Museum

Taharqa was also to face the growing power of the Assyrians at the border city of Ashkalon, where he won a short-lived victory. Only two years later (664 BCE) the Assyrians reached Memphis, capturing and deporting most of the Nubian royal family. Taharqa fled to Napata, the Nubian capital.[20] Once again Egypt was ruled by a remote foreign king who had little interest in Egypt and the ideologies of kingship which were fundamental to the Egyptian way of life. The Nubian rulers tried to re-take Egypt from the Assyrian overlords and Taharqa's cousin, Tanutamani, managed to recapture Aswan, Thebes and Memphis. However, this was quickly followed by an Assyrian assault, resulting in Tanutamani's exile[21] and the Assyrians maintaining their control of the Nile Valley.

During the conflict between the Nubian twenty-fifth dynasty and the Assyrian overlords, another dynasty rose to power. The Assyrian king, Ashurbanipal installed Necho (Nakau) (I) of Sais to rule Egypt as a puppet king, and his son Psamtik (664–610 BCE) ruled from the Delta town of Athribis. When the Nubian Tanutamani tried to regain control of Egypt he killed Necho but Psamtik managed to escape. Later that year Psamtik killed Tanutamani and his army, becoming the appointed king of Egypt by the Assyrians. In 653 BCE he broke the Assyrian link and ruled Egypt independently for 54 years.[22] Although the collapse of the Assyrian Empire benefited Egypt, it left a power vacuum which many nations tried to fill, resulting in Egypt fighting with the Persians against the Babylonians in 616 BCE. It was not entirely successful and a year later the Persian army defeated the Assyrians, becoming the new superpower.

Psamtik made many improvements during his reign least of all strengthening trade links, especially with the Mediterranean. He encouraged foreign traders to come to Egypt, especially Greeks as they were the purveyors of luxury items, using the increased revenue to build and repair temples.[23] Psamtik's son Necho II (Nekau) maintained particularly good relations with the Greeks, employing a number of Greek mercenaries in the Egyptian army; the Greek inscription on the leg of one of the Colossi of Memnon (plate 8) mentions two Greek regiments of the army.[24] Psamtik had rewarded mercenaries with strips of land on either side of the Pelusaic branch of the Nile, which they could farm and earn an income from. They would be expected, however, to be available to fight whenever required.[25] This meant there was an increased number of foreign settlers in Egypt, and during the later reign of Ahmose II (570–526 BCE) there was an Egyptian uprising against the privileged treatment of the Greek and Carian regiments over the Egyptian *machimoi* or military class.[26] By the reign of Darius II (423–405 BCE) from the First Persian Period, there was further conflict between the Jewish mercenaries on Elephantine in the south and the priests of Khnum, resulting in the temple of Yahweh being burned to the ground.

The foreign mercenaries, however, were essential to the Egyptian military and Psamtik also concentrated on building a navy. He commissioned a series of ramming battle ships known as triremes, using the expertise of Greek shipwrights at Herakleopolis Magna. It is thought these boats were used in both the Mediterranean and Red Sea[27] to combat foreign boats of similar design and they were connected to his increased trade with the Red Sea area. Necho, Psamtik's son, continued the work of his father maintaining and improving the navy which secured Red Sea trade, especially with the land of Punt. After the reign of Ramses III, records of trade with Punt ceased but incense, the most important export, was still required and the Red Sea gave access not only to Punt but also to the Sinai, where turquoise and copper were obtained. Necho commissioned a canal linking the Pelusaic branch of the Nile to the Red Sea, bypassing the traditional desert route:

> It was Necho who began the construction of the canal to the Arabian Gulf ... the length of the canal is four day's journey by boat, while its breadth is sufficient to allow two triremes to be rowed abreast ... The construction cost the lives of 120,000 Egyptians. Necho did not complete the work; he stopped in deference to an oracle that warned him that his work was all for the benefit of the 'barbarians' – the Egyptians term for anyone who does not speak Egyptian.[28]

Necho pre-empted the Suez Canal by 2500 years, and like the modern canal this was to prove to be lucrative for Red Sea trade, guiding the ships through the fortress of Pelusium. After losing 120,000 men to the project, Necho approached an oracle regarding the success of the canal (fig. 33). The oracle said the only people to benefit from it, should it be completed, would be foreigners. The canal was to be completed by Darius I in 497 BCE, in year 24 of his reign, which he recorded on four large stelae placed along the route, starting at Bubastis, travelling eastwards along the old Necho Canal into the region of Isma'iliyya. Before it reached Lake Timsaeh, it turned south-east, skirting the Bitter Seas and flowed west from the modern Suez Canal towards the south to Suez and into the Red Sea.[29] The inauguration of the canal was a lavish affair, with 24 Persian ships loaded with the taxes of the satrapy of Egypt, sailing from Egypt to Persia via the canal, and it is thought Darius himself oversaw the event.[30]

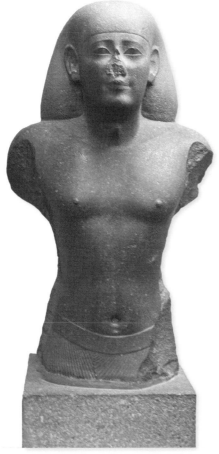

33 Saite King. British Museum

The accounts regarding the construction of the canal, however, are contradictory, with Herodotus claiming Darius completed it and Diodorus Siculus, Strabo and Pliny suggesting it was unfinished even in the first century CE, due to the discovery that the Red Sea was a higher level than the Nile.[31] It is thought these contradictory records were due to a misunderstanding; Ptolemy II did not complete it but rather dug it out after it had silted up and during the Roman period a change of water flow patterns in the eastern Delta led Trajan to move the course of the canal to flow by the Fortress of Babylon. Over the years the name changed from 'River of Ptolemy' to 'River of Trajan', but according to Islamic records Trajan's canal completely silted up and was reopened in 641–642 CE, remaining navigable until 767.[32] Even if there were contradictions regarding who built and completed the canal, it was clearly important and was used for nearly 1000 years.

Herodotus records that the completed canal could fit two trireme ships alongside each other, which could be up to 45m wide, running for a distance of 84km.[33] Archaeology of the site has shown that in the Wadi Tumilat region there were in fact three active canals, not just one, which merged in the vicinity of Tell al-Retabah. The northern was older than the southern canal and possibly ran the entire distance of the Wadi until it joined to the third waterway. However, none of the remains of the canal banks have been excavated, although in 1983 an archaeological survey identified the remains of a large settlement, but studies have shown it was probably seasonal, with the canals only being navigable during the times of high flood.[34] Whatever the exact course, Necho's canal was to prove invaluable for trade to the Red Sea, although the ships returning would be unable to navigate the canal with the winds and were likely to return via the well-trodden desert route. Even during the Roman and Ptolemaic period the cargoes were unloaded at the Red Sea and carried overland to Egypt.[35]

Although Necho did not complete the canal, he ensured the ships were safe in the Red Sea, clearing the area of pirates by placing his newly constructed triremes here to protect the cargoes on their journeys. These were the most up-to-date vessels and only the bravest pirates would attempt to attack them, although they had troubled Egypt for a while. Herodotus mentioned the Ionians and Carians first came to Egypt as pirates but were conscripted into the Egyptian army as mercenaries under Psamtik I.[36] These mercenaries were essential in the battle between Psamtik I and the Assyrians.[37]

The ambitions of Necho and his maritime activity developed into a legend recorded by Herodotus that he sent an expedition to circumnavigate Africa.[38] He sent several Phoenician ships down the Red Sea to the Indian Ocean, returning to Egypt via the Straits of Gibraltar after two to three years. When they ran out of resources the crew would stop, sow seeds and wait for the harvest before moving on again. The distance travelled is 24,140 km with an average sailing distance of

112km per day (only sailing during daylight hours). The winds and currents were also favourable, enabling such a voyage, although there are some scholarly doubts as to the truth of the tale. Although it was possible to carry out this journey in the time suggested, the three years recorded were viewed as an ideal number, putting this tale into the genre of propaganda.[39] At the time of Herodotus, contemporary geography and the size of Africa were great topics of debate, whereas such exploration was not a typical Egyptian activity unless there was purpose and gain to be had. Exploration for the sake of exploration was a Greek idea and Necho was placed into this role by Herodotus and other classic writers as an alternative to Persian rulers,[40] showing Egyptian superiority.

The increased trade links with the Red Sea and the Mediterranean saw the development of port towns whose main income was trade. Naukratis, for example, became a busy centre of industry, with a thriving trade in exports and imports and was perfectly situated for both internal and external trade;[41] it remained an important harbour until Alexandria was founded (331 BCE). Herodotus records that Ahmose II gave land at Naukratis to Greek settlers, either to live on or to build shrines on if they were to live abroad. This meant this city was viewed by some to be a Greek colony with a high number of Greek occupants.[42] Although primarily a trade post, Naukratis was also known for its pottery production, and the site has shown evidence of a faience factory, a shipyard responsible for boat repair[43] and the earliest evidence of iron-smelting, playing a key role in introducing iron to Egypt.[44] Naukratis was situated on the Canopic branch of the Nile and the winds at the mouth of the branch drove ships towards the town, which sat as an intermediary between Sais and the Mediterranean cities, being named the 'House of the Harbour'.[45]

During the reign of Ahmose II (Amasis) (570–526 BCE), Greek trading ships were obliged to pay taxes on their cargo before reaching Naukratis, and this was the channel by which all Greek vessels were forced to travel as they were banned from entering the other Nile channels. As the large Greek merchant ships were unable to fit down the Nile channel, they were obliged to unload onto flat-bottom Egyptian vessels for this part of the journey. The most valuable of Greek imports were silver and wine, and as Ahmose encouraged Greek traders, he applied Greek laws on the Canopic branch, indicative of the number of immigrants in this region.[46] This created a good alliance with Greece which was needed to fight against the growing power of the Persians. The innovations of Ahmose II ensured that his reign was particularly successful:

> It is said that it was during the reign of Ahmose II that Egypt attained its highest level of prosperity both in respect of what the river gave the land and in respect of what the land yielded to men and that the number of inhabited cities at that time reached in total 200,000.[47]

The crops grown through this period were similar to those that were always cultivated in Egypt, including emmer or hulled wheat, barley and flax which was popular with the Mediterranean traders.[48] Land during this period was distributed amongst the crown, the *machimoi* (the Egyptian military) and the priests, although the land owned by the crown was not as prominent in the records as in previous dynasties.[49] These lands were either worked by the palace staff or distributed in payment for services to palace officials or mercenaries. From the fourth century BCE grain was the biggest export from Egypt and classical reports mention Greek ships sailing from Egypt laden with grain[50] which brought a very high income to the seller.

Despite the hard work of Ahmose in securing international relations and strong trade links, his successor Psamtik III was not to be on the throne for long before he faced a Persian attack on the Pelusaic branch of the Nile. The power of the king throughout the Late Period had deteriorated until they were on the same level as the vizier, as is demonstrated on a seal from the reign of Necho showing the king standing side by side, as if equal, with men of official rank.[51] Members of the royal retinue were also buried alongside the Libyan kings in their tombs, something unheard of in the New Kingdom. This meant that when Psamtik III was faced with the Persians he had neither the experience nor the power behind him to repulse them. Cambyses led the Persian army to Egypt and met Psamtik III at Pelusium at the mouth of the Delta.[52] Consequently, in 525 BCE, after less than a year on the throne, Psamtik fled to Memphis, to be captured by Cambyses and transported to Susa, the Persian capital.[53]

The main records of the Persian conquest of Egypt are from classical authors and are grossly exaggerated due to Greek and Persian conflicts. The archaeological evidence, however, sees a gentle takeover at the time of the collapse of the Saite dynasty, with the Persians being particularly sensitive towards Egyptian religion and practices. Cambyses II (525–522 BCE) was said by Herodotus to have desecrated the body of Ahmose II, although evidence indicates he and his successor Darius I were sympathetic to the Egyptian way of life, adopting cartouches, worshipping local gods and restoring temples. Cambyses also resided over an Apis Bull burial at the Serapeum. He allowed the Egyptians to rule their country with a Persian satrap in control, whilst they governed remotely from Persia.

Although the First Persian Period was one of instability, it has produced the most valuable record of Egyptian history, that of Herodotus (c.484–c.425 BCE), a Greek historian who visited Egypt gathering information for his *Histories*. He spoke to numerous priests asking them about religion, lifestyle and history, and took everything he was told as truth, presenting a skewed view of Egyptian history. Egypt at this time was considered to be a place of great learning, and this reputation was to grow over the following centuries. Herodotus viewed Egyptian wisdom as second to none, even if he thought some of their religious practices were barbaric.

After 100 years of remote Persian rulers, the Egyptians revolted with Amyrtaeus of Sais (twenty-eighth dynasty 404–399 BCE) taking the lead and Nefarud I (twenty-ninth dynasty 399–393 BCE), ruling from Mendes in the central Delta, continuing the campaign. At Nefarud's death, Hakor (393–380 BCE) brought stability back to Egypt, allying himself once more with the Greeks who were enemies of the Persians. After his death in 380 BCE his son Neferud II took over but was quickly deposed by Nectanebo I, the governor of the Delta town of Sebennytos. He ruled for 18 years and defeated a Persian-Athenian attack. To strengthen Egypt's borders he made an alliance with Sparta and Athens, as well as maintaining Greek connections.

To further stabilise the Egyptian economy Nectanebo (fig. 34) increased tax payments, which were to go to the temples to be redistributed, improving the local and state economy. These tax reforms were recorded on a large stela which stated that the king would give to the temple of Neith at Sais one-tenth of the imports from the Greek traders, as well as a tenth of the goods produced in Naukratis and a tenth of all that lay in the royal treasury. This would clearly increase the wealth of the temple, which in turn would be distributed to the local population in the form of wages and rations and was, therefore, essential to the economy.

34 Nectanebo Sphinx,
Luxor Temple

Even without this improving economy the Persians were not to give up on Egypt due to its importance in the area, and it took three assaults before, in 343 BCE, Artaxerxes III invaded and occupied Egypt. Nectanebo II was on the throne at the time, and when he was defeated he was the last Egyptian to rule Egypt independently until General Naguib in 1952. During his reign he is reputed to have built fortifications along the Mediterranean coast and the north-east Delta to protect the borders from the inevitable Persian invasion. All access to Egypt was blocked by land and sea, and the mouth of each of the seven branches of the Nile in the Delta had large fortified towns preventing any access to the Nile.[54] The Persians were expected to attack by land and sea and the Egyptians needed to be prepared for it.

The Second Persian Period was only to last a decade, with the final king of the period, Darius III, allowing Alexander to take Egypt without bloodshed. However, during this decade there had been a great deal of destruction of fortified towns and looting of temples. There were none of the sensitivities of the First Persian Period and this period was characterised by vicious and violent rulers. The Egyptians were therefore glad to have Alexander the Great take control from the Persians, providing them with some stability, even though it spelt the end of their independence.

7

A RIVER
WITHOUT A SOUL

332–30 BCE

The arrival of Alexander the Great (plate 9) saw the end of the Second Persian Period and the start of the Ptolemaic period. This was an interesting time as there was a large influx of Hellenes to Egypt, seeing a divide within the population between the Egyptians and the Greeks that had begun under the reign of Psamtik I. This influx was to split the community further. The culture and religion changed to incorporate these new innovative ideas, whilst still maintaining an Egyptian element. Although there were now two cultures living side by side, they still had the same thing in common – reliance on the river Nile. However, it has been stated that the Ptolemaic use of the Nile was more functional and: 'The Nile became a river without a soul, a mere hydraulic system whose only purpose was to produce wealth.'[1]

Whilst the Nile was further manipulated to increase the agricultural yield, it was still essential for leisure activities as well as practical ones, and therefore was as essential to the lives of the Ptolemaic community as it was for those living at the time of the pyramids or even today.

Alexander the Great came to Egypt in 332 BCE on his way to Persia, accompanied by a team of engineers who were experienced in drainage work.[2] He visited the Oasis of Siwa and the oracle of Amun, who named him as the new king of Egypt. He was crowned at the temple of Ptah at Memphis, as was traditional, and was furnished by the Egyptians with a full five-fold titulary.[3] On his way back to the Mediterranean in 331 BCE he stopped at a small fishing village called Rhakotis, opposite the island of Pharos, and constructed a city on the site. Alexandria was now the capital city of Egypt until the Arab invasion in (641 CE). The city was one of 17 of the same name founded by Alexander the Great, but is the only one still standing.

When Alexander arrived he realised the good position of the site, with access to fresh water from the Canopic branch of the Nile and the Mediterranean enabling the transportation of wheat and natural resources from Egypt to the rest of his empire. The island of Pharos and Rhakotis was also defended by Lake Mereotis (Mariot) to the south, making it the perfect place for the new capital city. He joined the two islands with a causeway called Heptastadion, which divided the waters into the eastern and western harbours, with the eastern harbour housing a man-made port with palaces, gardens and government buildings.[4] This causeway over the following centuries was silted up, and now forms part of the land. The eastern harbour was very active during the Ptolemaic and Roman periods and its importance increased in the middle ages, undergoing a gradual decline in the Ottoman period with competition from the ports of Rosetta and Damietta, whose position at the mouth of two branches of the Nile meant they were directly linked with hinterland, making them more favourable cities.

Alexandria was a bustling Hellenistic city and it has been said 'Then, as now, she belonged not so much to Egypt as to the Mediterranean'[5] as the city was more Greek than Egyptian. Alexandria became a centre of learning with the construction of the Mouseion which housed the library boasting a copy of every book ever written. The *Letter of Aristeas* describes the vision of a universal library: 'Demetrius … had at his disposal a large budget in order to collect, if possible, all the books in the world … to the best of his ability, he carried out the king's objective.'

Alexander never saw his completed city as he left before it was finished, although Ptolemy I brought his body back to be buried there in a golden casket. This has never been located. Some are of the opinion that it may have been beneath the site of the mosque of the Prophet Daniel and Strabo records that a Ptolemaic king stole the gold coffin, replacing it with one of alabaster or glass.[6] In 828 BCE, when Venetian merchants smuggled the body of Saint Mark out of Alexandria, some scholars believe they may have been deceived, taking the body of Alexander the Great instead. If so, he currently lies under Saint Mark's in the Vatican.[7]

The Library of Alexandria is generally believed to have been built by Ptolemy I or II. The texts in the library were written in numerous languages, although the most common was Greek, followed by Egyptian. The search for literature for the library was instigated by the Ptolemaic kings personally and it is recorded that every ship arriving at the harbour was searched for books. These were then taken to the library to be stored and a copy was returned to the original owner. Ptolemy III is recorded as having stolen the original manuscripts of the works of Aeschylus, Sophocles and Euripides from the Athenian archives after he convinced them to lend him the texts to copy. He sent copies back to the archives, keeping the originals. Other manuscripts were bought legitimately and the largest book sellers were in Athens and Rhodes, and in some cases numerous copies of the same text were purchased in this way. The Mouseion was modelled on the schools of Aristotle and Plato[8] and it is often stated that Aristotle's library was deposited in Alexandria, leading medieval scholars to the conclusion that Aristotle taught in Alexandria.

The original library was situated within the grounds of the royal palaces and was under the control of the royal family. As the library grew, 50 years after it was constructed it was necessary to construct further buildings to deal with the surplus of books within the archive, which may have exceeded 700,000 volumes. Sadly, the library burned to the ground in 48 BCE, and although the Romans started to rebuild it, it never reached the capacity of the Ptolemaic period, although it was the best in the Roman world.[9]

Alexandria was also an important harbour area, dominated by the Pharos lighthouse, together with at least three pairs of colossal statues of a royal couple which stood up to 13m tall and were made of pink granite.[10] The lighthouse has long since disappeared beneath the sea, but we have records of its appearance from ancient texts (fig. 35). Abu Hamid Al-Gharnati visited the lighthouse in 1110 CE and described it as having three tiers, all of stone with a 'Chinese Iron' of 7 cubits (364cm) wide, which were metallic and polished to a shine, acting as mirrors. These reflected the sun warning ships they were approaching the harbour, but were also used to direct sunlight onto enemy ships to set alight the wooden craft.[11] Another medieval author, Ibn Hawqal, believed the lighthouse was used as an observatory to study astronomy.[12] Blocks recently discovered underwater from the lighthouse, each weighing in excess of 75 tons, indicate what a colossal structure this was.[13]

The water here has produced a great deal of evidence regarding the structures of the city and the harbour, as a series of earthquakes in 365, 447 and 535 CE, coupled with subsidence[14] and evidence of a large earthquake or tidal wave[15] has resulted in 4–7m of the coastline being submerged into the sea and, with it, much of the ancient city. Due to a bar of rock under the water, many Greek and Roman ships ran aground and sank some 350m from the lighthouse and the remains are still visible on the seabed, although due to subsidence the rock is now 7m lower. These wrecks are complete with wine amphorae, oil lamps, bronze vases and ship anchors, and give valuable information about trade during the Ptolemaic period.[16]

The remains of the original harbour serving Pharos was discovered by Jondet in the bay beneath the water, standing at 8ha in size with artificial walls 4km long.[17] There was a 160m landing quay 1.3m inside the present harbour.[18] Before the discovery of these remains, the only record of the harbour was in Homer's *Odyssey* (Book 4), and was believed to date to Ramses II or III, although others believed it could be an Old Kingdom structure[19] or even Cretan.[20]

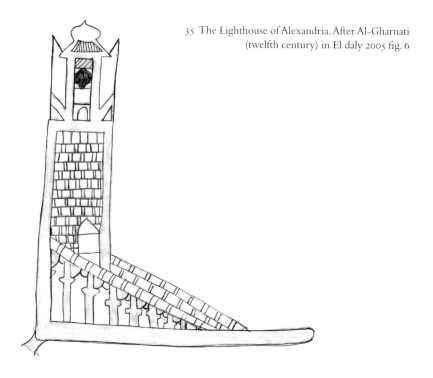

35 The Lighthouse of Alexandria. After Al-Gharnati (twelfth century) in El daly 2005 fig. 6

However, the harbour at Alexandria was not the only important port in the area, and Lake Mereotis (Modern Lake Mariot) to the south-west of the main city was connected to both the Canopic branch of the Nile and the Mediterranean through canals. It was the only fresh-water coastal lake in Egypt and was therefore an important agricultural area, with glass, pottery and wine production being important along its banks.[21] Evidence of cisterns, wells and *saqqia* (waterwheels) are also indicative of vineyards and wine production in the area. The lake originally covered an area of 50km and ongoing excavations along the shoreline have identified harbours, jetties and quays used for mooring boats, to load and unload cargoes, together with the remains of necessary warehousing. Access to the lake enabled any cargoes to reach both the Egyptian and Mediterranean worlds.

Underwater archaeology in the eastern harbour has also uncovered statues, pillars, sphinxes and structural blocks. There were hundreds of pink granite columns[22] sailed from Aswan to Alexandria using barges similar to those used by Hatshepsut for her obelisks. Some of the granite blocks were transported whole, whereas more evidence suggests other stones were cut on site before transportation and subsequent reuse.[23] A number of blocks and statues were dated from as early as the Middle Kingdom and had been moved from Heliopolis, where the temples were being utilised as a readymade quarry.[24]

Alexandria was dominated by water, with the Mediterranean acting as a natural northern border and numerous lakes situated throughout the city. Buildings were erected along the banks of the lakes, including a large temple constructed by Cleopatra VII. This temple was recorded in 1922 as lying between Nouha and Sidi Gabar on a road running by Lake Hadra, which has since been filled in and the newly-developed land built upon.[25] Maps from as recently as 1865 CE show the site was covered with sphinxes, statues and columns, with two colossal statues which once stood in the temple depicting Marc Anthony as Osiris and Cleopatra VII as Isis. Whether there was some significance to the close proximity of the lake for anything other than practical purposes is unknown, but it is likely that the water from the lake was used within the temples for rituals and purification.

The Nile and its subsidiaries were utilised in the religion of the Ptolemaic period even though the religion was changing; they incorporated Hellenistic characteristics and practices in addition to the changing roles of the most famous Egyptian deities. The temple of Philae is a prominent one of the period (fig. 36). Although constructed by Taharqa (twenty-fifth dynasty), it gained real prominence during the Ptolemaic period. It was built on an island associated with the 'Island of the time of Re',[26] indicating it was the island upon which all creation started. The temple was dedicated to the goddess Isis and remained in use until 550 CE, being the last temple to close. It is particularly interesting as the Nubian god Aresnuphis was also worshipped here as a companion of Isis, and the Mammissi here celebrated Isis raising Horus alone in the marshes after the death of Osiris. The mythology of Osiris and his death were celebrated at this temple with images of the gathering of his severed limbs as well as a chapel dedicated to Horus the Avenger. It was clearly an important site which was enlarged and improved by most Ptolemaic kings and Roman emperors.

During this period re-enactments and dramatisations became very popular, and these are recorded on temple walls. One such re-enactment was *The Triumph of Horus*, recorded at Edfu temple during the reign of Ptolmey IX (110 BCE), and it is believed it was performed annually at the Festival of Victory, on the twenty-first day of the second month of winter, daily for five days (9–13 January). The festival commemorated the wars between Horus and Seth, and Seth's ultimate defeat by Horus based on the *Contendings of Horus and Seth*. The re-enactment was carried out within the temple boundaries and was not for public entertainment, but a ritual emphasising the divinity of kingship. The entire 'play' concerns the continuing struggle between Horus (the king) and Seth, resulting in the king killing Seth and demonstrating his dominance over chaos, as well as avenging the murder of Osiris. Seth is represented as a hippopotamus, although due to the uncertainty of the outcome should a real one be used, this was symbolised by a cake. The king ritually thrust spears into the hippopotamus, leading to its destruction (fig. 37). The cake is then cut and distributed amongst the actors and priests. The re-enacted story is much older than Ptolemy IX, and there are scenes from the story presented at Edfu by earlier Ptolemys. It was clearly an important festival, essential for the continuation of the divine king. As much of the play was performed on water it was probably acted on the sacred lake, representative of the primordial waters of creation. This lake was filled naturally from sub-soil water as most of the sacred lakes were, and was affected by the water levels of the inundation. At the time of the celebrations the Nile would be at a low level, six months before the inundation began.

Although the re-enactments were popular, they did not replace the traditional Nile procession, and in the Festival of the Beautiful Reunion during the third month of the season of harvest (15 April–15 May) the goddess Hathor travelled in her sacred barque, named the *Mistress of Love*, from Denderah to the temple of Horus at Edfu, over 100 miles to the south. The journey took four days by river and was joined by various temples who added boats to the procession. On the first day of the journey, Hathor stopped at Karnak, visiting the shrine of the goddess Mut. On the second day, the procession stopped at the sanctuary of the goddess Anukis at Per-Mer, and on the third day Hathor reached Hierakonpolis, where the procession of the local Horus accompanied her on the rest of the journey to Edfu. Before she reached Edfu, Horus of Edfu and Khonsu left their temple to meet the procession of Hathor part way and escort her to the temple. The statues of Horus and Hathor were placed together in the shrine for a period of 14 days, to enable them to celebrate their 'marriage'. The focus of this festival was fertility and rebirth, symbolised by the divine coupling of the deities. For the two-week period, which was accompanied by offerings, rituals and celebrations, the city was described as:

36 Philae Temple

1 Sunset over the Nile at Luxor

2 The Holy Family in Egypt. Hanging Church, Cairo

Left: 3 Scorpion Macehead. Ashmoleon Museum (*Courtesy of Brian Billington*)

Below: 4 Pleasure Lake from the tomb of Nebamun (eighteenth dynasty). British Museum

Opposite page

Above: 5 Sacred lake at Medinet Habu

Below left: 6 The golden mask of Psusennes from Tanis. The Ancient Egypt Picture Library

Below right: 7 The silver anthropoid coffin of Psusennes from Tanis. The Ancient Egypt Picture Library

Opposite: 8 Greek graffiti on the leg of the southern colossi of Memnon

Left: 9 Alexander the Great. (*Courtesy of Photos.com*)

Below: 10 Ibn Tulun Mosque, Cairo. (*Courtesy of Brian Billington*)

Left: 11 Islamic Cairo at night

Below: 12 Battle of the Pyramids. (*Courtesy of Photos.com*)

Bottom: 13 Champollion defaces a pillar with his name at Karnak

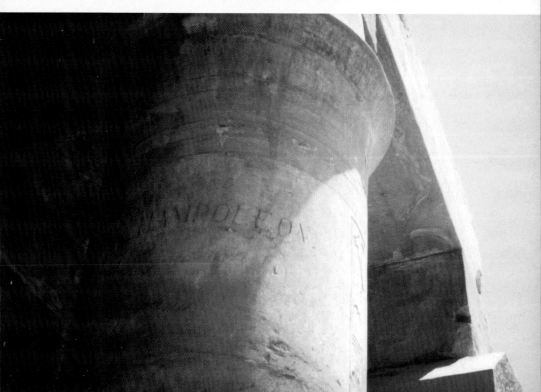

14 Thomas Cook tour poster. (*Courtesy of the Thomas Cook Archives*)

15 Temple of Debod, Madrid. (*Courtesy of Photos.com*)

37 Triumph of Horus, Edfu

bestrewn with faience, glittering with natron and garlanded with flowers and fresh herbs. Its youths are drunk, its citizens are glad, its young maidens are beautiful to behold; rejoicing is all around it and festivity is in all its quarters. There is no sleep to be had in it until dawn.

Once the festivities were over, Hathor returned to Denderah in another riverine procession, accompanied by priests, musicians, dancers and the general populace lining the riverbanks, hoping to catch a glimpse of and be blessed by the goddess.

Water also featured strongly in the cult of Osiris from Canopus, a town near Abuqir, 19km to the east of Alexandria,[27] on the mouth of one of the seven distributaries of the Nile. The Canopic branch of the Nile was called the 'Great River' or 'Great Spirit' by Herodotus, Strabo and Ptolemy,[28] and has since dried up. Of the seven distributaries, only Damietta and Rachid (Rosetta) still flow.[29] The Canopic branch of the Nile was the only one during the Ptolemaic period that could be navigated by ships, and was therefore essential for trade and so instrumental in the success of Canopus. It remained an important distributary until the ninth century CE.[30] In the Ptolemaic period an artificial canal was dug between the Canopic branch of the Nile and Alexandria, making travel between the two easier and trade more efficient.

The inhabitants of Canopus held particular favour for the cult of Osiris, represented by human-headed jars (fig. 38). The Greeks record the cult claiming the hero Kanopos, the helmsman for Menelaeus, was worshipped at Canopus in the form of a jar, and these were depicted on some Roman coins, minted in Alexandria. Early Egyptologists, seeing the heads of the jars and reading the name from the coins, made the assumption that 'canopic jars' were the same as the jars that held the preserved organs from hundreds of burials. The name has stuck even though we now know that canopic jars have nothing to do with the cult of Osiris of Canopus. The jars in the cult of Osiris were often dummies where the lids were moulded to the base, but were symbolically believed to hold Nile water and were carried in procession by priests. By the Roman period the cult had spread to Memphis and figures in the round representing Osiris-Canopus have been discovered.

During the Ptolemaic period, the Nile continued to be used for practical and leisurely activities, and Appianus of Alexandria (c.95–165 CE) and Gaius Suetonius Tranquillus (c.69–post-130 CE) record that this was combined in 47 BCE when Cleopatra VII and Julius Caesar went on a Nile cruise from the capital in Alexandria to Upper Egypt. Some have speculated that at this time Cleopatra was pregnant with Caesar's child,[31] representing the ideal couple, although some conflicting reports state Caesarion, Cleopatra's son, was not born until after the death of Caesar, indicating she conceived on a two-year visit to Rome in 46–44 BCE.[32] This Nile trip, albeit partially for pleasure, also had a very practical purpose, enabling Cleopatra to repair her relationship with the people of Middle and Lower Egypt after the damage caused by her brother/husband Ptolemy XIII. It was also a means for Cleopatra to show that Egypt was supported by Rome, which could be viewed as positive or threatening. The journey may have borne the appearance of a victory parade which had been carried out for centuries as the royal barge was accompanied by 400 ships crewed by Roman soldiers. According to Lucan (65 CE), Caesar also had a personal interest in the journey as he was hoping to be able to locate the source of the Nile:

> Despite my strong interest in science, said Caesar to Acoreus, Priest of Isis, nothing would satisfy my intellectual curiosity more fully than to be told what makes the Nile rise. If you can enable me to visit the source, which has been a mystery for so many years, I promise to abandon this civil war.

It is thought that this cruise may not have been as extensive as perhaps Caesar would have liked, and it is likely they sailed no further south than Thebes or possibly Memphis.[33] Once they returned to Alexandria, Caesar was satisfied that Egypt would be safe with only a rudimentary military presence and left for Rome, leaving only three legions behind.

After Julius Caesar's death his successor Octavian also embarked on a riverine tour of Egypt, but with a more heavy-handed approach that Julius. The Nile was the easiest way to visit all areas of Egypt and provided an easy means for transport of goods to Alexandria and then Rome. Initially Octavian travelled from Alexandria to the south, inspecting canals and irrigation channels, ensuring the agricultural land available was maximised to provide Rome with as much grain as possible. He also wanted to suppress the animal cults which were popular in Egypt, refusing to visit the Apis Bull of Memphis. This did not endear him to the Egyptian people, but little did he realise that the priests of the Apis Bull had already commissioned a relief depicting him performing the rights to the god.[34] According to Egyptian artistic and religious ideas, this depiction was tantamount to the offerings actually being performed.

Living in Alexandria, Cleopatra was clearly comfortable with boats and sailing, and this is no more apparent than in her first official meeting with Marcus Antonius in 42 BCE. The murder of Julius Caesar caused a break in Roman leadership and the empire was divided among Caesar's great-nephew Octavian, who later became Augustus, Marcus Lepidus and Marcus Antonius (Marc Antony), who became a great love in Cleopatra's life. Marc Antony summoned Cleopatra to Tarsus (Turkey) to question her on her loyalties following the murder of Julius Caesar when she was visiting him in Rome. As a shrewd politician, she only agreed to meet him on Egyptian territory and sailed to meet him just off shore. He was invited to her boat to dine. Plutarch describes the vessel:

> A barge with a gilded stern, purple sails, and silver oars. The boat was sailed by her maids, who were dressed as sea nymphs. Cleopatra herself was dressed as Venus, the goddess of love. She reclined under a gold canopy, fanned by boys in Cupid costumes.

38 A canopic jar, Canopus. (*Courtesy of UCL, Petrie Museum of Egyptian Archaeology UC48023*)

Antony, it was claimed, was impressed by her blatant display of luxury, just as Cleopatra had intended, and tried to out-do her in extravagance the next evening. Antony was enthralled with the young queen and travelled with her to Alexandria spending the winter of 41–40 BCE with her. Their revelry at this time was recorded by Plutarch (110 BCE–15 CE) with a hint of disdain. He records that eight boars were roasted for a dinner of only 12 people, one after another, so a perfect meal would be ready whenever Antony and Cleopatra decided to dine,[35] displaying extravagance and waste that was not received well in Rome:

> She played at dice with him, drank with him, hunted with him; and when he exercised in arms, she was there to see. At night she would go rambling with him to disturb and torment people at their doors and windows, dressed like a servant-woman, for Antony also went in servant's disguise … However, the Alexandrians in general liked it all well enough, and joined good-humouredly and kindly in his frolic and play.[36]

The relationship between Antony and Cleopatra was clearly one of frivolity; she shared all of his activities, inviting criticism from both the Roman and Egyptian people, who believed such leaders should display appropriate behaviour. However, although she lived this frivolous lifestyle, Cleopatra exercised control over Antony which she used for political advantage. She convinced him to give up the Alexandrian lifestyle and continue his campaign to annex Parthia, as this would strengthen his position in the Roman triumvirate, benefiting both Rome and Egypt.

Although the relationship with Rome was important and time consuming for the Ptolemaic rulers, a great deal of effort also went into internal policies, especially that of agriculture and subsistence. These are well documented from various sources, including the Zenon Archive from the reign of Ptolemy II. Zenon was the manager of a large estate at Philadelphia in the eastern Fayum, and records his ongoing concern with irrigation.[37] The other group is the Petrie Papyri – fragments saved for recycling which were destined for cartonnage. These texts, coupled with archaeological excavation, tell us a great deal about the agricultural process. In the first three reigns after Alexander, land reclamation was particularly important and there was extensive construction of new dykes, canals and drains,[38] and the records show plots of 10,000 arouras of land (2700ha) reclaimed in the Fayum alone. Working on the land was not paid well and the farmers, farm hands and labourers were at the lowest end of the pay scale. Most of the farmers were the native Egyptians, and some enterprising people rented additional land from a landowner with no taste for farming, earning extra income.

All land ultimately belonged to the crown and was classified loosely as royal land or remitted land which was worked by various groups of farmers.[39] Land tax was a complex issue during the Ptolemaic period, with various people of status being exempt from certain taxes, whilst others were subjected to myriad taxes. For example, Alexandrian landlords were exempt from crown and harvest taxes,[40] whereas farmers were taxed according to the crops grown. There were two types of crops: subsistence crops of the type grown throughout Egyptian history, and cash crops introduced by new immigrants to Egypt. The subsistence crops were taxed in kind, whereas the cash crops were taxed in metal. The immigrants did not have any problems paying this, nor in paying the investment in planting these crops. In the 1960s Egyptian farmers commented that they would rather grow subsistence than cash crops: 'Why should I buy my bread when I can grow it myself?'[41] This seemed to be the sentiment during the Ptolemaic period too, as most of the cash crops were farmed by immigrant workers rather than native Egyptians.

The main subsistence cereals were emmer and barley which were both used for beer, the staple drink of the Egyptians. Just prior to Alexander the Great, the Greeks introduced husked emmer (*Olyra*), which lost popularity and was replaced with durum wheat (*sitos*).[42] Other subsistence crops included cabbages, lettuces, cucumbers and other vegetables, herbs and figs. Evidence from the city of Karanis, in the north-eastern Fayum, shows a varied landscape comprising fruit and nut trees, including date, fig, hazelnut, walnut, pine, olive, peach, Indian medlar, quince and pistachio, as well as vegetable crops of radish, lentils, barley and wheat.[43] These would have formed the basis for the Egyptian diet at this time.

Cash crops made up all vineyards and it is recorded that there was a manual on viticulture combining the new agricultural venture with the love of knowledge which characterised the Greeks. Vineyards in the Fayum were planned together with works on drainage and irrigation,[44] and were therefore very much imbedded in the water management systems of the region. The Revenue Laws Papyrus[45] of Ptolemy II describe how one-sixth of the tax collected on vineyards and orchards was to be sent to the cult of Arsinoe at Philadelphous, his deceased sister and wife, the exemption being only those situated on temple land.[46] As the economy of Egypt was based on distribution, the temples remained the centres of this system; food from the temple stores would be distributed to the local community in the form of rations and wages.

These cash crops were more important to the economy, and whereas most villages boasted a resident brewer and vintner, not all villages had a baker.[47] Such crops were centrally controlled and a schedule has survived describing records of crops to be sown and harvested with estimations of rent to be collected.[48] Further evidence in the form of taxation documents and land registers emphasise the abundance of produce[49] and the successful irrigation programmes in place, with even low Nile floods having minimal impact on their well-organised regime.

These cash crops were distributed to all parts of Egypt, especially Alexandria and Lake Mareotis (Mariot), to be exported to Greece and the Near East. This distribution was carried out on large cargo ships, manned by corvée labour, prisoners, slaves, criminals or young men press-ganged into joining, which was banned by the Rosetta Decree,[50] and crew members were then paid for each journey made. As the work was undesirable there was a high level of desertion in the Ptolemaic navy, and when they were recaptured and transported back to base, Papyrus Hibeh (2.198) records that some were branded[51] to make recapture on a later date easier. Evidence suggests the lower ranking soldiers were normally native Egyptians whereas the captains and officers were Greek. As this work was considered objectionable, in addition to being paid, the crew members were also exempt from other forms of corvée labour as an incentive to join. Due to the high desertion level and the unreliability of the sailors, private landowners hired their own sailors and, in the Zenon archive, Zenon is asked to hire some men for transportation of some dignitaries but he is advised to 'Take a description of the Sailors' which would enable him to trace them should they disappear.[52]

Not all of the Ptolemaic army, however, were so unreliable, and for the early part of the period the army followed Macedonian practices and were successful in their endeavours. However, by the reign of Ptolemy IV the army structure was beginning to deteriorate with an increase in the employment of mercenaries. There was also a large reserve army living amongst the community. The navy was not the Ptolemaic army's strong point, although it was essential if they were to be successful in the Aegean and Eastern Mediterranean, and it reached a high point in the late fourth century BCE. The most famous battle was the Battle of Salamis off the east coast of Cyprus in 306 BCE under the reign of Ptolemy I. The Egyptians had 140 warships against 180 of the enemy. The battle techniques employed were the same as those on land, with the gradual decline in manoeuvres as ramming enemy ships became more popular.[53] The Egyptian fleets suffered a great defeat at Salamis, losing half the fleet, although they were later to be successful on land at Gaza.[54] In 267–261 BCE the Chremondean War saw the Ptolemaic army, led by Ptolemy III, fight the Macedonian navy, which led to the Egyptians securing some new island bases.[55] This naval victory, however, was to be followed by further seaborne defeats at Ephesus (258 BCE), Cos and Andros (245 BCE), reducing the islands under Ptolemaic influence.

Trade relations during the Ptolemaic period were vast, and their expansionist activities included Greek centres in the Mediterranean, India and Syria–Palestine. Trade with the latter was so common that in the minds of the Egyptian inhabitants Syria and Egypt were almost linked. In a prophetic dream of Hor of Sebbenytos (168 BCE), during the reign of Ptolemy VI when Egypt was threatened by external sources and the political infrastructure was deteriorating, he dreamt of Isis walked across the Syrian sea until she reached the harbour at Alexandria where she declared the city would be safe.[56]

The Ptolemys were successful in their endeavours until the end of the third century BCE, when all Ptolemaic influence in Greece had declined, with only a single garrison on Thera remaining.[57] This necessitated a number of port sites along the northern coastline and the Red Sea. One such Red Sea port was Marsa Nakari, linked to the Nile via the ancient road to Apollinopolis Magna (Edfu). Along this road archaeological excavations have uncovered gold mines, quarries, forts and watering places.[58] This port was possibly founded by Ptolemy II and was in use until the Islamic period. During the Roman period it was connected by a land route to the port of Berenike a little further south on the Red Sea coast, which was instrumental to their trade with India, meaning Marsa Nakari was used as a way station. During the Ptolemaic Period, excavations have shown that wine, glassware and stone quarried in the eastern desert were exported from Egypt and beads from India and Sri Lanka were imported via this route. As this was a particularly small port, it benefited from a fortified enclosure surrounding it, the tower of which may have served as a signal platform for incoming ships.[59]

As with all periods of Egypt's past, the Nile was a fickle friend and there were times of high or low floods which were disastrous to the inhabitants. From the Ptolemaic period we have evidence of the procedures put in place to deal with these potential problems. Should the dykes breach, the local nomarchs arranged men to repair them and organised the corvée labourers to maintain the canals throughout the year.[60]

The Fayum papyri record that during the inundation there were dyke guards on duty and engineers were on call with shovels, baskets and jars in case the dykes should be breached. Water management at this level was the responsibility of everyone from the king to the farmer,[61] and all would help during hard times. It was managed on a local scale. However, in 245 BCE, during the reign of Ptolemy III, the Nile flood became too high resulting in destroyed crops, meaning that Egypt had to centrally import grain.[62] Even if the floods were acceptable, the soil quality for planting crops was also a problem then as it is now, with salination being a particular concern. Zenon makes reference to this in one of his letters: 'We are weeding the poppy and the wheat. But reckoning it up we find that some thirteen arouras only have poppy and the rest has salted up.'[63]

It seems that the Ptolemaic period was also a difficult time for the farmer, living hand-to-mouth and being totally reliant on the inundation for survival. This is something that was not to change in the next 2000 years, even when there were political and environmental changes which were to alter the culture and future of Egypt. The end of the Ptolemaic period was one such event. In 30 BCE, at the death of Cleopatra VII, Octavian Caesar occupied Alexandria thereby ending the gradual collapse of the Egyptian Empire and the country was completely absorbed into the Roman Empire. However, although Cleopatra is often blamed for its downfall, it was a long decline to reach that point and from the reign of Ptolemy III there was civil unrest in Egypt due to extensive taxation, and from the reign of Ptolemy IV external forces were taking advantage of Egypt's political weaknesses. During this reign a number of ports and land possessions had been captured by rival kings at a time when Egypt was not politically strong enough to defend them.[64] The early Ptolemys were an unstable family, with assassination common between rival siblings, husbands and wives, or children and their parents for the throne. It was just such a rivalry which eventually led Julius Caesar to the doors of Cleopatra, as he facilitated in a conflict between her and her brother/husband Ptolemy XIII.

The Egyptian population, especially the Alexandrians, were frequently retaliating against foreign rule, including strikes, attacks on villages and temples, even to the abandonment of entire villages. This has been interpreted as a reaction to famine and hardship,[65] perhaps caused by bad flood levels and over exploitation of the land for the purpose of trade and exportation. The reigns of all the Ptolemys are peppered with tales of the Alexandrian mob breaching the palace or forcing an unpopular king into exile. Cleopatra VII tried to appease the people by preventing such exploitation of the Egyptian workforce though the issue of a decree (41 BCE):

> A complaint having been brought before us by people of this city, particularly those that operate agricultural domains in the Prosopite and Bubastite nomes – on the pronouncement of the judgement of 15 Phamenoth against the civil servants of the nomes – the objects of the complaint being the way in which these last, against our policy and instructions many times communicated by those responsible for the finances, in accordance with or decision that no one is allowed to exact from these people anything more than the duly established royal taxation, manage to tax illegally, adding those people to the roll of the agricultural and local levies, which do not concern them at all judging, because of the hatred which in the past we dedicated to such abuses.[66]

Whilst Cleopatra tries to solve this issue of farmers being over taxed illegally she absolves herself from any guilt, placing the blame upon the local nomarchs and administrators indicating such matters were locally governed. However, by getting involved in the issue she is trying to win favour with the lower-class Alexandrians which would aid her reign. Nonetheless, it was all to be in vain, as even with the support of the Egyptians and the Alexandrian mob, her love affair with Antony led to some bad decisions which put her life and the future of the Egyptian nation in peril. Her short lapse of judgment at the Battle of Actium laid Egypt's defences bare, resulting in the occupation of Alexandria by Octavian Caesar and Egypt's annexation into the Roman world.

8

THE CROSSROADS OF
THE WHOLE WORLD

30 BCE–641 CE

The Romans were involved in Egyptian politics from the Ptolemaic period, primarily for financial reasons, and when Egypt became part of the Roman Empire in 30 CE this intensified. However, access to Egypt and its resources was restricted and even the senate was not involved in the administration – senators even being forbidden from visiting Egypt without permission from the emperor.[1] A governor was appointed to deal with Egypt's administration, while the emperors remained in Rome. Very few of the Roman emperors ever visited Egypt, choosing to govern remotely even though general tourism was popular, with Romans travelling to Egypt on Nile cruises, visiting the pyramids at Giza, the Labyrinth at Hawara, the Theban temples and the Valley of the Kings. The Colossi of Memnon was a popular stop-off, especially at dawn when the statue would 'sing' as the sun rose (fig. 39). They were thought to represent Memnon, the son of Eos, the goddess of dawn, whom he greeted each morning. The northernmost statue emitted a sound like a harp string breaking as the sun warmed it up. The tourists left graffiti over the legs of the statue recording their experiences: 'I came at night to listen to the voice of the very divine Memnon, and I heard it, I, Catulus, chief of the Thebiad.'[2] When Emperor Septimius Severus visited the statue was silent so he had it repaired, and it has not 'sung' at dawn since.

As we learned in chapter 7, Julius Caesar travelled the Nile hoping to discover its source, and this in particular was a Roman curiosity and a saying in Rome 'Quaerere Fontes Nili' stated that to look for the source of the Nile was like looking for a needle in a haystack.[3] Like the Greeks before them, the Romans were keen to locate it but were not successful. King Juba II, who was married to Cleopatra Selene, the daughter of Cleopatra VII and Marc Antony, claimed to have discovered the source, supporting this by producing a crocodile from the source, which was presented as a votive offering to the temple of Isis of Caesarea.[4]

39 The Colossi of Memnon, Luxor

Augustus (Octavian) Caesar visited Egypt in order to evaluate the resources, irrigation systems and agricultural land. Hadrian's (117–138 CE) visit spanned 8–10 months, visiting every area of Egypt; another partaker in the Nile cruise. This visit almost bankrupted Oxyrhynchus in the Fayum, who provided food for him and his retinue comprising 1000 litres of barley, 3000 bundles of hay, 372 suckling pigs and 200 sheep.[5] Whilst in Egypt, Hadrian founded the city of Antinopolis in 130 CE, the only town founded by the Romans in Egypt.[6] Antinopolis (modern el-Sheikh 'Ibada), near Hermopolis Magna, commemorated the drowning of Hadrian's favourite, Antinous, in the Nile nearby.

Although little of the city remains today, it was designed in the Greek style, with the streets at right angles. There was a triumphal arch, marked by two corinthian columns, public baths and a theatre. The gateway to the theatre marked the southern end of one of the main streets running parallel to the Nile. The original gate, made of iron-plated wood, was removed to Cairo and hung at the great gate of Bab Zuwalila. The city maintained its importance and in the Byzantine period it was the capital of the Thebiad.

The Roman period in general was a time of continuity rather than innovation, and the practices of the Ptolemaic period were maintained.[7] For example religion during the Roman period followed the Ptolemaic religious practices, and amalgamated Egyptian deities with Roman ones. This type of adaptability was characteristic of the Egyptian religion, perhaps explaining its longevity. The religion of Egypt was stable until the third century CE, when the Roman Empire was weakening and the temples were not as wealthy as they had been previously. The Roman emperors, however, were prolific temple builders and Alexandria alone had more than 2000. The most popular deity was Isis, who was sometimes associated with Hathor, but was always represented as a mother and faithful wife – an idea very close to the heart of all good Romans (fig. 40). She protected the activities of all women, including prostitutes, and was worshipped all over the Roman Empire. Whilst she adopted a Roman appearance, the practices remained Egyptian and the waking of her statue and adornment with jewels was one of the most important aspects of the daily rituals.

Other gods were adopted into the Greco-Roman pantheon for specific functions, such as the Greek god Pan who was associated with Amun-Min, an Egyptian fertility god. Koptos was the cult centre of the god Min, and this was extended during the Roman period. Koptos was the start and end point for trade coming from the Red Sea and for roads across the eastern desert. Amun-Min/Pan became the god of the eastern desert, guarding these routes, and was depicted with an incense burner, symbolising the spices and imports from the east.

40 Roman Isis. Naples Museum

As with religion, agricultural practices were also adopted from the Ptolemaic period or earlier. Roman Egypt was divided into 30 administrative nomes, inherited from the Ptolemaic era, reduced from the Pharaonic 42. Each one had its own governor, answerable to the prefect or regional administrators, as well as its own capital city. In the Roman period, however, most of the land was privately owned, although there was still some owned and farmed by the state. A number of lease agreements have been discovered from the town of Tebtunis in the Fayum, indicating that fields were rented out normally for two or four years at a time. The rent depended on the crops grown, with a higher price, normally in kind, for a food crop like wheat or barley, and a lower one, normally in cash, for fodder crops. The latter was often charged in advance; possibly because of the difficulty in predicting the market price on fodder.[8] The leases specified one year would be a cereal crop and the following year a fodder crop, demonstrative of the typical crop rotation pattern in place. The tenant took responsibility 'to complete the customary work as appropriate',[9] financing the cultivation and was obliged to provide labour or to sublet. Some tenants needed loans in order to finance this, but would only have problems paying back the loan should the Nile and consequently the crops fail. This enabled the landowner to ensure his land was farmed without the chore of having to cultivate it himself.[10] This system remained in place throughout the Coptic and Byzantine periods, although the land was divided into small-holdings, worked by a small number of full-time farmhands and numerous part-time temporary workers,[11] who were paid monthly salaries in grain.[12] It is clear from the number of lease agreements discovered that agriculture was a major source of income in the Fayum, and water management was therefore essential.

Arsinoe (Crocodopolis), in the Fayum had devised a system of running water supplied by two reservoirs into which water was lifted from the Nile,[13] and the governors of Arsinoe also introduced a centralised transport system in order to distribute crops and produce to the rest of Egypt and abroad.[14] The records from the Fayum indicate the irrigation was used primarily for cash crops rather than subsistence crops, while experimental crops such as poppies and olives, planted and nurtured from pips,[15] also taking advantage of the advanced water management systems here. Strabo commented on these olive groves:

> This nome is the most remarkable of all in its appearance, its fertility, and the way it has been developed. It is planted with olives and is the only area to grow large, fully grown olive-trees which bear a fine crop; and if the crop were collected in carefully it would produce good oil too … and it produces plenty of wine, and grain, pulses and may other kinds of crops.[16]

The vast estates of Appianus in the north-west Fayum in the third century CE, as recorded in the Heroninos Archive, were administered by wealthy town councillors and landowners of the estates, and farmed by a nucleus of full-time workers supplemented by extra labourers when needed.[17] The main purpose of his land was the production of wine, and it was planted with orchards and vine-yards which by their nature needed careful water management and to be situated on land free from the inundation, either on the desert margin or on higher land above the flood plain.[18] This land required artificial fertilising by spreading animal dung and canal silt[19] as well as manual watering, which was therefore very labour intensive for the maintenance of the crops. Other crops, such as vegetables or summer crops, on the other hand, were planted on late-draining land low on the Nile banks, benefiting from uncontrolled or free-flowing water, meaning very little manual watering was required.[20] These crops were cultivated for food for employees, fodder for animals and grain for tax.[21]

The irrigation dykes for such agricultural ventures were carefully monitored and the Charta Borgiana Papyrus (192 CE) describes how, in the Fayum town of El Lahun, their maintenance was carried out by corvée labour during the months of February and March.[22] This ensured that during the inundation only the required amount of water reached the agricultural land. Such localised con-trol of the irrigation dykes and the distribution of water to the large estates and landowners in the region meant it was in their best interests to ensure the water reached all of their land, as during the Roman period the Nile floods were lower than they had been during the Ptolemaic period.

To monitor the rise of the Nile, Augustus Caesar completed a Nilometer, started during the Ptolemaic period, at Elephantine in the temple of Khnum. It was a rec-tangular well cut into the rock, lined with sandstone blocks 11.25m deep.[23] Demotic and Greek inscriptions within the Nilometer show there was once a balustrade sur-rounding it and a terrace where beer makers sold their produce to visitors.[24] The Nilometers were essential to the economy, as predicting water levels using these gauges meant taxes could be calculated; a good flood meant a good crop and higher taxes. Pliny, in his *Historia Naturalis*, defined what these levels were:

An average rise is one of seven metres. A smaller volume of water does not irrigate all localities and a larger one, by retiring too slowly, retards agriculture; and the latter uses up the time for sowing because the soil is parched. The province takes careful note of both extremes: in a rise of five-an-a-half metres it senses famine and even at one of six metres it begins to feel hungry, but six and a half metres brings cheerful-ness, six-and-three-quarters complete confidence and seven metres delight.[25]

The importance of utilising every drop of water, especially during low floods, saw the introduction of the *saqqia* (waterwheel) (fig. 41). Although the *shadduf* was cheap to run, the amount of land it could irrigate was limited, and was only really effective with trees and vines that were planted in straight lines with a small channel running between them. The *saqqia* meant larger areas could be irrigated with less effort.[26]

The agricultural production of the Nile Delta and the Fayum were essential to the Roman economy, and was supplemented by gold mining and porphyry quarrying in the eastern desert.[27] Egypt was known as the breadbasket of Rome, and Augustus Caesar commissioned an annual shipment to Rome of 170 million litres of grain, about 10 per cent of the entire Egyptian harvest. The Egyptians got very little in return for their corn and grain, and it was more taxation than trade.[28] Corn ships left Alexandria in May or June bound for Rome and, as they were travelling against the northerly winds, this could take up to two months, along the North African coast or north to Cyprus, hugging the south coast of Turkey. Bad weather could ground the ships in Athens where people would stare in awe at the boats:

> What a size the ship was! Fifty-five meters in length, the ship's carpenter told me, the beam more than a quarter of that, and thirteen metres from the deck to the bottom, the deepest point in the bilge … The crew must have been as big as an army. They told me she carried so much grain that it would be enough to feed every mouth in Athens for a year.[29]

The return journey took about two weeks and Emperor Gaius commented that they travelled 'with the speed of racehorses'.[30]

Egypt was also a great provider of flour which could be transported and used for a variety of food products. It was ground using rotary querns and more commonly the level or olynthian mill, which have been found in Naukratis, Tanis, the Fayum, Quesir el-Qadim and the forts of Tiberiane and Mons Porphyrite, showing the widespread production of flour for both practical and trade purposes.

Egyptian exports, in addition to grain and food stuffs, were important, especially pearls, pepper, silks, frankincense, myrrh, spices and exotic medicines. These items were brought by ship across the Indian Ocean to the Red Sea coast and then to Koptos, floated to Alexandria and on to Rome. India, in return, received glass, textiles, wine, grain pottery, precious metals and people.

Stone was a major export, especially purple porphyry from Mons Porphyrite and the granite quarries in Aswan. The blocks, once cut, were loaded onto barges and floated to Alexandria where they were transferred to large ships (*lapidariae naves*) strong enough for such a cargo and sailed across the Mediterranean. As quarries such as Mons Porphyrite were located away from the Nile Valley, it was essential that the workers were supplied with adequate food and water. The Romans became adept at digging wells, utilising fossil water which abounded in the desert, and at the quarries and along the desert route from Berenike to Koptos

41 Nineteenth-century *Saqqia* (waterwheel). (*Reproduced with permission of the Griffith Institute, University of Oxford*)

such watering places (*hydreumata*) were dug every 20–30km. Mons Porphyrite was abandoned at the end of the Roman Period as imperial porphyry became unfashionable.[31]

Egypt was particularly known for its textiles, and woollen mills may have been situated at Antinopolis and Panopolis. Alexandria was the centre of the linen trade, made from locally grown flax as well as the reworking of oriental silks.[32] Along the Nile, the Delta and the southern shore of Lake Mareotis, various potteries with kilns produced a type of amphora jar which has been discovered in all Roman sites in Egypt.

Cargoes leaving Egypt were huge, comprising goods not only from Egypt but also from the Near East, India and Nubia. As Egypt was a pivotal point between these areas, ensuring safe passage on the Nile, the desert routes and the Red Sea was essential. This was aided by such documents as the *Periplus Maris Erythraei*, a sailing guide to the Red Sea, the Gulf of Aden and the Western Indian Ocean from the first century CE. It was reported that the best time to leave Egypt was July, with the south-westerly monsoons driving the ships over the Gulf of Aden and the Indian Ocean. However, the return was not possible until November, when advantage could be taken of the north-eastern monsoon winds.

In order to facilitate the trade routes, towns in the eastern Delta became trade centres. One such site was Pelusium (Tell el Farama), situated on Egypt's eastern boundary. Excavations were started there in 1992 as this area was threatened by the construction of the el-Salaam Canal. These excavations uncovered a number of late Roman (late sixth century CE) public buildings including a theatre and fortress, although it was inhabited much earlier. As this area was a departure point for expeditions to Asia as well as an entrance into Egypt, it was well protected and the fortress was huge, covering an area of 20 acres, comprising 36 towers, three gates and walls over 2m thick. Although this appeared to be indestructible, during the Persian invasion of 619 CE the fortress was razed to the ground.[33]

However, at its height Pelusium was a bustling harbour city with quays, magazines, customs offices, industrial areas, salt vats, textile workshops, pottery kilns, fish tanks, military installations and public facilities such as baths, theatres and racetracks. Excavations in the craft centre of Pelusium uncovered green slag from glass factories, detritus from pottery and brick making, and texts indicate the biggest product of Pelusium was salted fish and garum (fish sauce). Dyed linens were also very popular at this site and numerous myrex shells have been discovered here (snail shells used to produce purple dye which was particularly popular in imperial Rome). For such a productive area a reliable water supply was needed and the Romans constructed large tanks which were possibly used for water storage. These tanks may have started life as *saqqia* systems but the floors were replaced, turning them into tanks where large amphora and bucket-shaped instruments were used to remove water. They were possibly fed from shallow pools and drains nearby, and would have filled with water during the inundation, stored and used for the remainder of the year. Evidence of how these tanks fit into the wider scheme of agriculture and water management in the area is uncertain. The city was inhabited throughout the Roman, Coptic and Islamic periods until the reign of Saladin (1169 CE) when it fell into obscurity.

Alexandria was still the capital city during the Roman period, and had a large port with access to the Mediterranean and Red Sea, leading to the Indian Ocean and possibly even Malaysia and China.[34] Dio of Prusa writing in the first century CE commented:

> Alexandria is situated, as it were, at the crossroads of the whole world, of even its most remote nations, as if it were a market serving a single city, bringing together all men into one place, displaying them to one another and, as far as possible, making them of the same race.[35]

The fortress of Nikopolis, 5km east of the Alexandria's centre, together with the fortress of Pelusium, was well placed for the military to move to eastern trouble spots should the need arise, as well as to deal with the Alexandrian mob who had caused so much trouble during the Ptolemaic period.[36]

Augustus Caesar placed an army of 20,000 troops in various parts of the country,[37] with one legion at Nikopolis, another at Babylon in Cairo and the third in Aswan,[38] responsible for securing the southern borders and the desert regions. The eastern desert was a particularly dangerous place, thick with bandits attacking caravans from the Red Sea, and an additional string of fortresses between Berenike and Koptos was constructed along with watchtowers on the road between Quesir el Wadim and Koptos.

The migrating Nile dictated where towns and buildings were constructed as well as how they developed or diminished. The northward shift of the Delta base and the decreasing flow of water led to the silting up of the Pelusaic branch of the Nile in the eastern Delta, meaning all settlements on that branch relocated.[39] The landscape of Roman Egypt was totally different to that of today, and a Demotic text from the first century CE refers to an 'island in the middle of the land of Mennefer [Memphis]'. These islands may be mounds of land rising from the water after inundation or indications of the changing landscape of the Memphite area.[40] The Roman harbour wall was discovered here by Joseph Hekekyan in 1852, near to the ruin field of Koms Arba'ain and Nawa, showing that the Nile ran through what is now an inland area. Between the Roman period and the modern day the Nile has moved 3km east at Memphis. Diodorus Siculus (first century CE) records that a temple of Ptah (Daidalos) stood on 'One of the islands off Memphis' and later refers to a 'place opposite Memphis where the Nile divides and makes an island large enough to hold a very large army', indicating that the landscape we see today bears little to no resemblance to the marshy area dominated by canals, springs and islands of varying sizes upon which temples were constructed.[41] Studies in the area have also shown that the valley floor in this region has risen over 3m.[42]

The fortified town of Memphis and the fortress of Babylon were considered twin fortresses and both originally stood on the Nile (fig. 42). The construction of the fortress of Babylon was dictated by the local topography, and shafts dug 10m deep show there was a channel running north–south through the fortress, in use in the first millennium BCE, thought to be part of the canal originally built by Necho linking the Nile with the Red Sea. However, Trajan carried out some alterations, moving the mouth of the canal to Babylon and counteracting the silting up that was occurring in the original location.[43] It is believed that the canal was not extensively used due to northerly winds blowing from the Red Sea for most of the year, creating a hazard for Roman ships. Most chose the safer overland routes.[44] Trajan increased these land routes with a series of roads and harbours linking the Mediterranean with India, Jordanian trade routes, Red Sea coast and Sinai quarries in an attempt to increase revenue for Rome through trade.[45] The entrance was the same when built as it is today, flanked by two round towers, and remained an important site even after the Roman period and formed the centre of the early Islamic capital of El Fustat. At this time the entrance of the canal was blocked with a large wall and it was eventually filled in and built over. The line of the wall between the two towers and the date of structures built over the reclaimed land indicate the canal was still flowing in the seventh century, and some literary sources go as far as to suggest it was flowing until the ninth or tenth centuries CE.

42 Fortress of
Babylon, Cairo

Towards the end of the third century the Roman Empire underwent some changes which left it politically weakened and saw the introduction of Christianity. The beginnings of Christianity in Egypt are not clear as there is little information about its pre-Constantine form.[46] Egypt was fundamental to the development of Christianity although most Christians are unaware or ignore this. Many aspects of the religion were formulated in Egypt from the Nicene Creed: 'I believe in one God, the Father Almighty, Maker of all things both visible and invisible, and in one Lord Jesus Christ, the Word of God', to the canonical form of the New Testament;[47] the texts rejected by the Orthodox Church included the Gospel of Judas,[48] a somewhat controversial apostle, and the Gospel of Thomas.[49] Some believe Christianity was brought to Egypt by Saint Mark during the reign of Nero (54–68 CE), who was martyred in Alexandria. His body has since been moved to Saint Mark's church in the Vatican.

It is believed, therefore, that Christianity started in Alexandria and spread to the rest of the country through the Jewish community. By the end of the third century CE the Christian faith was fully developed and due to the political instability of the Roman Empire the people were willing to accept a new religion that could answer their problems. The political uncertainty, increased taxation, civic duties and conscription led to many leaving their villages (fig. 43) to reside in caves and tombs in contemplation of spiritual matters, seeing the start of the anchorite movement.[50] This became an important aspect of Christianity in Egypt, and Saint Paul (d. c.341) and Saint Anthony (251–356 CE) are both known for this lifestyle (fig. 44). Paul was the first hermit and Anthony the first monk, both of whom left their homes separately to live in the wilderness. Anthony was answering Christ's command to 'sell thy goods and feed the poor',[51] and started his journey by living in a tomb near his village, wrestling with demons and matters of spirituality.[52] It would be essential for these acolytes to settle near streams for survival, but for food they would have been reliant on Bedouins and pilgrims. Anthony became so famous that groups of people gathered to hear him speak, and the Emperor Constantine even wrote to him asking for his prayers to be answered.[53] At this time there were no organised monastic communities and this was the only way of obtaining spiritual guidance.[54] From the fourth century numerous monasteries had opened throughout Egypt which, like other structures, were located according to the Nile course. Saint Pachomius, for example, founded a monastery in 323 CE on the Island of Tabenna: 'But the shifting course of the river has long since annexed the island to the mainland.'[55]

Five Coptic monasteries constructed between the time of Constantine's accession (274–337 CE) and the Islamic invasion (641 CE) were originally built on a sliver of land sandwiched between the desert and the river, providing isolation and protection as if they were built on islands. Monasteries were mostly self-sufficient, cultivating their own lands, producing saleable objects and helping local communities by distributing alms to the needy and helping the sick. For extra income the monastic lands were also rented out, normally to richer members of society for cultivation.[56] The number of monasteries quickly grew and replaced the temples in the Egyptian distribution and subsistence system.[57] As the pagan temples fell into disuse and were forcibly closed, they were reused as monasteries and churches. This often necessitated a great deal of damage to the ancient wall reliefs as many of the figures and hieroglyphs were carved out, with crosses engraved in their place (fig. 45). Less destructive Christians plastered over the original reliefs, preserving them underneath, simply painting their Christian symbols and images over the plaster. As the plaster has since crumbled away the original reliefs are now visible.

Christianity was accepted by the Egyptians due to similarities with the traditional religion, with the expectation of an afterlife, and the reverence of a holy family: Isis, Osiris and Horus or Mary, Joseph and Jesus. Indeed many of the early images of Mary show her suckling Jesus and the imagery is identical to statues of Horus and Isis. In the treatment of Christian martyrs in the second century CE, the Osiris myth was called upon as their dead bodies were symbolically drowned before being preserved as relics.[58] Al-Maqrizi (d.1442), an Arab scholar, records one particular ritual at the Coptic Festival of the Martyr where the finger of a saint was placed in a sarcophagus and thrown into the Nile to assure a good annual flood.[59] There is a similarity between these rituals and the Osiris myth, where he was drowned in the Nile and later his penis was thrown in the Nile and devoured by a fish.

Symbolism such as the holy trinity and the cross or ankh were also comparable to the Egyptian religion, meaning it was not considered difficult to comprehend. Some aspects of traditional Egyptian religion and festivals also found their way into the Coptic calendar, in particular 'The Night of the Drop', where the rise of the Nile was celebrated on 17 June, when, according to doctrine, the archangel appealed to the Lord to raise the river.[60] In later times, the Muslims also celebrated the rise of the Nile, calling it *Munadee el-Nil*, 'Herald of the Nile'.[61]

The censuses of the second and third century did not record Christians, so it is difficult to identify their number, although it is estimated that the population growth of Christians was 3–4 per cent a year (40 per cent a decade), with only 1000 in 40 CE but forming the majority by the end of the late fourth century.[62] By the end of the third century CE there were churches in most areas of Egypt and there were bishops in most nomes with the episcopal throne situated in Alexandria. It was seen as the seat of all religious debate and controversy[63] and was one of the most prestigious cities of the period,[64] governing Christians throughout Egypt, the Sudan and Ethiopia. The Ethiopian church was always seen as a daughter of the Egyptian church and remained so until 1948.[65] The connection with Ethiopia settled into what was considered a mutually dependant relationship. Egypt relied on Ethiopia for the Nile silt from the inundation, and the Ethiopian Christians relied on the Coptic Church of Egypt for the patriarch selected to be stationed in Ethiopia.[66]

Above: 43 Byzantium village, Kom el Dikka, Alexandria

Left: 44 Saint Anthony. (*Public Domain on Wikicommons*)

Above left: 45 Coptic Archway, Dendera

Above right: 46 The Serapeum, Alexandria. (*Courtesy of Brian Billington*)

The church developed its own language and script, using the Greek alphabet to write Egyptian sounds, and it is believed that the Coptic spoken today is the closest one will get to hearing the ancient Egyptian dialect. The Coptic priests were considered by many to be scholars and 'wise men', and some monasteries acquired large libraries of biblical texts and theological works.[67] Emperor Theodosius (379–395 CE) started a campaign against paganism, although by this date there were not many pagans left in Egypt. He outlawed paganism in Egypt and destroyed texts, closed temples, barred the use of the Demotic language and the pagan holidays that were not adopted by the Church were made into working days.[68] The Bishop of Alexandria, Theophilus, took the opportunity to mock and provoke the pagans, who rioted in retaliation. The pagans barricaded themselves in the Serapeum in Alexandria (fig. 46), whilst Theophilus summoned monks and the Alexandrian mob to attack them. Their barricade was broken and they were slaughtered, and the last surviving books from the Alexandrian library were burned.

Only the temple of Isis at Philae was still functioning when Justinian (483–565 CE) became emperor, and it was finally closed in 535 CE. Philae has the last known hieroglyphic inscription, and upon its closure the ability to read and write hieroglyphs was lost to the world for over 1000 years. However, until the seventh century CE, scholars approached the monks and monasteries to interpret hieratic and hieroglyphic texts as they were the only ones still able to read it.[69]

Although conversion to Christianity was possible, and an option most Egyptians took, it was difficult and there was a period of instruction before one could be baptised into the faith. This led some to see Christianity as secretive, only open to the initiated, as well as being an uncompromising religion that wanted to win converts from paganism. It was therefore treated with suspicion by the Roman emperors. Decius (c.250 CE) persecuted the Christians throughout the empire, and Diocletian continued this in 303–5 CE.[70] It was so horrific that it is known in the Christian calendar as the 'Era of the Martyrs', of which there were many, all fundamental to Christian legends.[71] One such legend concerns the body of the martyr Saint Menas, which was carried by camel on procession. The camel suddenly stopped at what is now Abu Mena refusing to go any further; this inability to move a body is taken as a sign that the person wants to be buried where they stopped. Saint Menas was buried here and a spring appeared, which was considered a miracle and brought thousands of pilgrims to the site.

Christian persecution ended with Diocletian's successor Galerius, when in 312 CE an imperial policy of religious toleration was declared on the Edict of Milan, making Christianity a legal faith which could be professed publically. This resulted in a power struggle in Rome which was only resolved when Constantine the Great, a Christian, gained control in 323 CE.[72] This saw the start of the Byzantine period of Egyptian history (323–641 CE), which derived its name from the town of Byzantium on the Black Sea coast – the site of a new city founded by Constantine, called Constantinople. This site was fed by Egyptian grain and soon overshadowed Alexandria, becoming the new centre of trade in the Eastern Empire.[73] The grain which had been shipped to Rome was now diverted here.[74] Perhaps because of this, for the first time in centuries Egyptians were rising to positions of power as church leaders, representing their country on Church Councils.

The head of the Egyptian church was based in Alexandria and was a key player in international Christianity. However, in the Council of Chalcedon in 451 CE it was stated that the Church of Constantinople was secondary only to the pope, undermining the influence of the Alexandrian church leaders, leading them to break away from the Church of Constantinople.[75] The Constantine Church did not wish to lose the influence of Alexandria and sent a patriarch (*melkite*) to govern the Alexandrian church. However, the Egyptians did not want a foreigner as the head of their Church and lynched the first *melkite* who arrived in Egypt. This conflict had repercussions throughout Egypt, resulting in Nubian troops invading Upper Egypt. Constantine tried unsuccessfully to regain his stronghold but to no avail, and it was not until Emperor Justinian, in the fifth century CE, secured Egyptian defences and reorganised the administrative system so that Egypt was under Roman influence once more. His administrative changes secured the grain supply annually exported from Egypt to Constantinople and Rome.[76] This grain supply was threatened in the second half of the sixth century CE and the first half of the seventh century CE with continuing Nile failures, resulting in food shortages, as well as the gradual subsidence of the eastern Delta which reduced cultivation in Egypt by half. Egypt then suffered an outbreak of plague in 542–600 CE, so by the time the Arabs invaded in 641 CE its population had declined to 2.5 million,[77] leaving them demoralised and desperate.

Not long after the plague epidemic ended, the Persians gained a stronghold in Alexandria (619 CE), whilst the population was at its weakest, governing Egypt for the following 10 years. The eastern emperor overthrew Persian power throughout the empire, but this was to be short lived and the Byzantine governor of Egypt was confronted by the Arab general, Amr Ibn Al-As, in 640 CE,[78] at the death of Mohammed. The Arabs first defeated the Byzantines in the Fayum (640 CE) and then the fortress of Babylon (641 CE). The Egyptians, in their weakened state, were pleased to lose the yoke of the Byzantine rule and welcomed the Muslims, hoping these new invaders would be an improvement.

🏺 9 🏺

RIVER OF PARADISE
AND RECEPTACLE OF
THE RAINS OF HEAVEN

641-1798 CE

The Arab general, Amr Ibn Al-As, led his army to victory against the Byzantine rulers of Egypt in 641 CE.[1] A series of battles, beginning in 639 when the Arabs reached Egypt, led to the fall of Pelusium in 640, followed by Babylon in April and Alexandria in November of 641. The final annexation took place in 644 CE during the Caliphate of Umar, when an army of 4000 Muslims marched upon the fortress of Babylon.[2] From this beginning, Egypt's Islamic history becomes complex, with different families, nations and groups controlling Egypt: the Fatimids from 909–1171 CE, the Ayyubids until 1250 CE, the Mamluks until Egypt became part of the Ottoman Empire in 1517, who were conquered by Napoleon in 1798.

By the time of Egypt's annexation in 644 CE most of the population were Christian and were seen as 'people of the Holy Book' by the Muslims, and were therefore under their protection. As long as they paid the ever-increasing taxes, the Christians were safe from persecution. There was no real incentive to convert Christians to Islam as the government would lose the large taxes inflicted upon non-Muslims. Initially there was very little change to urban or rural life in Egypt, as the new rulers were content to allow the Egyptians to govern the way they always had. However, this was not to last long, and one of the first changes the Muslims made was to place names, starting with the name of Egypt itself. Egypt was now named Misr after the grandson of Noah, meaning country, urban centre and border. Four further towns were named after Misr's sons, Sa, Atrib, Ashmun and Qiftim, giving the modern names of Sais, Athribis, Ashmunein and Qift (Koptos). Qifti was also the name given to the Copts and subsequently all native Egyptians. Today the Copts are believed to be the true descendants of the ancient Egyptians.

It would appear that this initial inertia was due to the early Muslim invaders not realising the true value Egypt held:

Most merits of Egypt are brought to her, so much so that someone even said the four elements are brought to her; water which is the Nile is brought from the south, the soil is brought in the water otherwise is it only sand that does not grow plants, free from wood which is imported into it and air/wind blows from one of the two seas, the Rumi and the Qulzum. [Mediterranean and Red Sea][3]

The importance of the fertile land, however, was quickly realised, and between 641 and 776 CE there was a labour crisis when they had more land than available labour.[4] This was exacerbated by extreme taxation, resulting in the desertion of entire villages as a means of tax evasion. All land belonged to the Islamic state, managed by the caliph, and worked by labourers to raise taxes.[5] In 727–728 CE, in order to increase farmed land and revenue from taxes, the state relocated Arabs from Syria to the eastern Delta, hoping that with extra manpower they could double the amount of land farmed and crops harvested. This system was unsuccessful as the Copts in Upper Egypt waged war against tax officials, and in 737 and 739 CE the relocated Arabs joined the revolt, refusing to pay the exorbitant taxes.[6] These uprisings continued until 794, when tax officials were expelled from the new capital, Fustat, by the settled Syrians. The state backtracked by 776–795 CE but the taxation laws were still different for Muslims and non-Muslims. Land held by Muslims was subject to the 10 per cent or tithe payment, whereas non-Muslims paid more. The state also recorded that Egypt had been taken by force, whereas it had been conquered by treaty. If the land was taken by force it was subject to double the rate of taxation, and the Islamic state took advantage of this. Farmers were finding it harder to meet these increasing taxes from the crops they were growing.

The crops grown were varied and the Survey of Nabulsi (1245 CE) describes farming in the Fayum and the taxation on each crop type. The area was abundant in vineyards, gardens, date-palms, figs, olives,[7] sesame, flax and indigo – all cash crops used for export and trade.[8] The most prominent cash crop, however, was sugarcane, and a great deal of land was saved for this crop. Processing the sugarcane was also dealt with in the villages and many had their own ox-drawn stone presses.[9] Less common in the Fayum were sustenance crops of rice, cumin, vetch, fava beans, barley and rape. The Fayum, due to its fertile soil, maintained its cash-crop estates which had been established in the Ptolemaic period. The water management systems in place to irrigate the various crops included canals, irrigation channels, sluice gates, weirs, *saqqias* and water-sharing partnerships between neighbouring villages.

The crops grown in the Fayum would be shipped to the new capital city at Fustat,[10] near the fortress of Babylon in Cairo, for distribution and export. This was the only large city left in Egypt as the others, like Memphis and Alexandria, had fallen into disrepair.[11] Initially it was used as a military encampment, and evidence shows these early soldiers were of the Yemenite tribe. It soon expanded and became a bustling metropolis, secondary only to Baghdad, with one travel writer, Ibn Hawkal (tenth century), describing market places, gardens and six-storey houses.[12] Excavations have discovered the residential area with houses of bricks and mortar, decorated walls and stone floors. The houses were surrounded by animal pens, stores and silos,[13] indicating that many of the inhabitants were wealthy. The Nile used to run alongside the town, although this was slowly migrating eastwards, and the town migrated northwards as new suburbs became prominent, which included al-Aksar (a military town of the Abbasid period) and al-Qatai (Tulunid period).[14]

In 972 CE Al-Qahira (Cairo) was founded, enclosed within large mud-brick walls, overshadowing the smaller town of Fustat. Within the enclosure walls were palaces, pavilions, houses, offices, baths, gardens, fountains, the mint, arsenal and stables, and it was reserved for the caliph, his chosen officials and military. However, people from Fustat worked within the walled city of Cairo but were forced to leave each evening by the Bab Zuweila gate (fig. 47). Although now secondary, Fustat remained an important city as it served the caliph and the elite and became a trade link between Cairo and the rest of the outside world.[15] Trade and exportation were essential to the Islamic economy and the largest exports in medieval Egypt were textiles[16] and raw flax.

By the eleventh century, flax production in Egypt served markets at home, Europe and North Africa,[17] and records show that one merchant, Ibn Awkal, may have shipped over 700 bales of flax of approximately 90kg each in a single year. A quarter of these bales sold for 4860 dinars at a time when an average middle class family earned 2 dinars a month. The large quantities of flax required, inflated its price in local farming areas, so farmers were not only able to name their price but also demand payment, not in standard dinars but high quality gold coins. Records indicate there was even a 'bureau de change' in the market place at Abusir, at the stall of Ibn Yasir, indicating that various currencies were accepted in such rural areas. The textiles of Egypt were so famed they were responsible for providing the *kiswa* (curtain) which covered the *Kaaba*, the focus of the hajj from 1258 CE,[18] and a long caravan left Cairo annually on pilgrimage. The Egyptian sultan was not only responsible for the safety of the caravan to Mecca, but also benefited from providing them with everything they needed for the journey.

During the Mamluk period (1250–1517 CE) trade relations existed between Egypt and Byzantium, Aragon, Genoa, Venice, India and the Far East, with large quantities of saris, silks and spices entering Egypt via the Red Sea which were exchanged for glassware and ceramics. The Red Sea ports were linked to the Nile by overland routes, the most commonly used being to Koptos (Qus), which had

47 Bab Zuweila gate, Cairo. (*Courtesy of* ARCE)

been in place from the pre-dynastic period. The trade for gold and black slaves from Nubia was strangely carried out via the Red Sea and the overland route to Koptos, rather than the land or Nile route from the south through Aswan, and may have been part of a wider exchange network where the Red Sea ports were one of many stops. The slaves were destined for the harem, agricultural work, domestic servitude or the military.[19] In the Ottoman period (1571–1798 CE) coffee was newly imported to Egypt, and Cairo was the centre of the coffee trade between Yemen and Europe, with most Cairo merchants storing or transporting the beans.

With such extensive river traffic travelling from Koptos to Fustat and then onwards to Alexandria, it was important to carefully monitor the Nile and the inundation. In 715 CE a Nilometer was constructed by Soliman on the southern end of Roda Island (fig. 48),[20] which was joined to Fustat by a bridge of boats and also to Giza by a second bridge. Ibn Tulun sometime later (876–877 CE) built a fortified redoubt near these bridges as a safe haven for his wives and treasury; these were to be flooded and destroyed by the inundation.[21] The tendency for the island to flood made it perfect for the Nilometer, which comprised a three-storey well, some 13m deep, with three openings at different levels leading to the Nile and a central marble pillar with a scale marked in cubits (fig. 49). When the Nile reached 16 cubits, the inundation began, at 18 cubits the middle lands flooded and at 20 cubits the high land was irrigated.[22] It was only once the water rose to a sixteenth of a cubit on the Nilometer that tax was calculated and often the government lied about the height in order to start the annual taxation.[23] During the early Islamic period (641–776 CE) taxation was based on administrative districts, divided locally by village leaders between different households depending on their ability to pay. Tax was paid in kind or in cash, and was assessed in the autumn based on the Nile flood. The district's taxes came from the spring harvest based on previous years with the same Nile levels.[24] This collective taxation often resulted in collective tax evasion. People suspected of tax evasion were imprisoned, even if the harvest failed and they did not have the crops with which to pay. From 795–827 CE rent was collected in addition to tax, and was expected to be paid in cash, although it was often paid in kind.

The ninth century saw a series of high floods resulting in the silting up of the eastern branch of the Nile and the shift of the riverbank westwards,[25] but low floods were the real concern and for 26 years between 622 and 1200 CE the floods failed, causing famine and severely diminishing the economy. Records from the flood of 963 CE describe how the cost of wheat inflated and people starved. Ibn Zahitah stated one of these famines lasted for three years, during which time the king waived all taxes, collecting double when the Nile rose again.[26] The famines were disastrous for the economy, affecting everyone, not just food producers.

Al Baghdadi reported that during the famines of 1200–1202 CE, of 900 weavers in Cairo only 19 survived.[27] As non-food producers, they relied on bartering for food and were unable to produce any for themselves should there be none to buy.

This constant threat of low flood waters was exacerbated by the Egyptian relationship with Ethiopia. In 1089–1090 CE the Arab writer al-Makin reported the Nile failed and it was rumoured the Ethiopian emperor had built a mound blocking the Nile. The sultan sent the Christian patriarch, Michael of Alexandria, to Ethiopia, requesting the Ethiopians restore the stream. The Ethiopian monarch of the Zaguie dynasty ordered the mound of earth to be broken, resulting in the Egyptian Nile rising 3 cubits in one night.[28] During the reign of the Emperor Lalibala (1172–1212 CE) the idea of diverting the Nile in order to 'famish Egypt' was introduced as retaliation for Muslims invading and chasing the Ethiopians from their land. Lalibala was hoping the Nile could be 'directed into the low country southward', not reaching Egypt. This idea of diversion ended with Lalibala's death, and evidence of the excavations have never been discovered. Somewhat later, the Ethiopian emperor, Zar'a Ya'qob (1434–1468 CE) threatened the Egyptian Muslims with making the Nile fail if they continued persecuting Ethiopian Copts. He claimed the only thing stopping him was his fear of god and the suffering that it would cause.

48 Roda Island Nilometer, Cairo. (*Courtesy of Sonia Brasseur*)

49 Roda Island Nilometer, Cairo. (*Courtesy of Sonia Brasseur*)

This hostility escalated to the realms of mythology with the Frenchman Phillippe of Mezières (1330), who reported that an unnamed Ethiopian ruler diverted the river causing a drought in Egypt, frightening the Egyptians so much they allowed the Ethiopians to travel through their land without paying taxes. This story of diversion remained a threat in the minds of the Egyptians until the eighteenth century. Henry Salt, however, commented that the only 'source of the river' Lalibala had control over was a Nile tributary, the Takazze, near Lasta,[29] which limited the power they had over the Nile itself. The Ethiopians could never have affected the Nile inundation, at least not until the modern era and the introduction of dams and dykes through the southern stretch of the Nile. In 1618 CE the Jesuit writer Batazar Tellez examined the landscape of Ethiopia and declared the diversion of the Nile would be impossible, and by the early eighteenth century this idea had been totally rejected in Europe.

Despite these concerns about the Ethiopians, water management in Egypt was very advanced, with the construction of a series of five aqueducts of varying altitudes from 4–50m above sea level.[30] The first surviving aqueduct was constructed in 680–690 CE under Governor 'Abd al 'Aziz Ibn Marwan, of fired bricks with earth or mortar joints. The second aqueduct (Abbasid) was built from 750–765 CE and was a large arched structure ending in a cistern with arches and small elongated apses. In 870–880 CE this aqueduct was modified, cut off from the cistern and redirected to the aqueduct of Ibn Tulun (868–884 CE), providing water to his palace at Habal Yshkur (fig. 50). Several arches are still extant between Birkat el Habash and the palace. The Ibn Tulun aqueduct was built to supply Fustat with water. He paid for its construction, his new city Al-Qatai with his mosque in the centre (plate 10), and a hospital after discovering 4000kg of pharaonic gold. All that remains of Al-Qatai is the mosque, which is the largest and oldest in Cairo. He then decreed that no one could hunt for ancient gold without state permission and accompanied by a state official.[31] Many such treasures were thought to be protected by the waters of the Nile, and there were spells 'On lowering the waters' to reveal the treasures beneath,[32] although control over the treasure hunters developed into a guild under the Fatimids,[33] severely limiting who could search for it.

The fourth aqueduct was built by the Fatimids in 973 CE, and belonged to a network of aqueducts and cisterns expanding over the south-east of Cairo.[34] The fifth aqueduct was built after 1095 by Vizier al-Afdal for his master Sheikh al-Atfihi. It drew water from the aqueduct of Ibn Tulun, although the slope of the water had been changed in 870–880, now running from east to west. This was destroyed towards the end of fourteenth century.[35]

50 Ibn Tulun Aqueduct. (*Courtesy of the Creswell Archive, Ashmolean Museum, Oxford, and Harvard College Library Archive ICR 0708*)

Although they were quite advanced in water-management techniques, religion was still used to explain some aspects of the Nile and the environment. The inundation as central to the fertility and success of Egypt made it into the legends of the medieval period, and Al Wahrani records that as punishment from God, a pharaoh's throne was sunk into the earth and was only visible when the Nile dropped very low. This was possibly used to explain how the island at Giza emerged from the waters.[36] Such islands were always rising from the waters due to the migrating course of the Nile and the distribution of silt which formed islands and joined islands to the mainland. Medieval authors indicate that the problem of the migrating Nile was as big an issue then as it is now, although they suggest it was exacerbated by the people themselves, as the Nile was used to dump rubbish which changed the shape of the banks and affected the flow of the Nile over the years. As the banks of the Nile were piled high with debris it altered the patterns of flooding, silting one bank more than the other.[37] Abu Salih 'the Armenian' (twelfth-century) records that many houses and churches were built on areas of land free from the annual floods but were subsequently flooded due to the changing course of the Nile, showing an unpredictability in its course even on a local scale.[38]

These early Muslim scholars separated the world into two periods, that of pre-flood and post-flood. The flood was thought to have happened in 3100 BCE, some 3671 years before Islam, coinciding with the founding of the first dynasty,[39] indicating the flood was viewed as a time of creation and new beginnings. This indicates that even in Islamic Egypt the Nile was celebrated as a holy river[40] and the myth of Osiris, Seth and Isis made its way into Arabic folklore and popular magic. In the Arabian epics of Al-zir Salim, his sister saved his body by floating him out to sea in a wooden chest reminiscent of the watery death of Osiris. Following Osiris' drowning, in the ancient myth his spirit became trapped in a tree which was then used as a pillar in the palace of the king of Byblos, and some modern Egyptians still believe trees grow from the bodies of saints. The Osiris bed, associated with new life, placed into tombs to pinpoint the moment when the deceased was reborn, is still practised in a fashion in modern Egypt when, on 25 July, seeds are sown on a plate and their growth represents new life.[41] Isis also finds herself morphed from Egyptian, into Christian and then Muslim religion. She was equated with the wife of Moses, Asia, whose name was derived from Isis, and is thought to be buried near Ibn Tulun's mosque, which became a holy pilgrimage site.[42]

A number of medieval pilgrims continued worshipping the Egyptian god Imhotep under the Quaranic form of Joseph, recorded as receiving divine revelations whilst imprisoned in the Memphite necropolis, the cult centre of Imhotep. Muslims considered Memphis as the site of an oracle, where God answered requests and Imhotep healed ailments.[43] The Greek Hermes was also closely associated with Imhotep and in Arabic folklore he was said to be the first astronomer, builder, doctor and poet:

> The first to predict the Flood and to foretell that a celestial catastrophe of water and fire would strike the earth, and he became concerned that science and other forms of knowledge would be lost; so he built the pyramids that can still be found in Upper Egypt. On the wall of the pyramids he drew, all forms of technical equipment and devices and described all aspects of science, intending to preserve them for future generations, because he was afraid that they might be lost to the world.[44]

Hermes or Hermes the Copt, as he was later known, was the source of all scientific knowledge, and followed in the footsteps of Thoth the ancient Egyptian god of knowledge. Hermes was believed by the Arabs to be not only the god of knowledge but also the founder of the science of alchemy, a great interest of the medieval scholars.

However, Hermes' ability to predict the annual floods was of great use and interest to all Egyptians, who believed various superstitions regarding the flood. Ibn Duqmaq (d.1406) describes an ancient idol which was thought to protect them for excessive floods: 'A talisman to keep the Nile within its banks. It is said that the statue known as Abu Al-Haul (the Sphinx) at the pyramid, is aligned with the above idol, both facing east.'[45]

The Sphinx was considered a powerful god, even during the Islamic period, and Al Idrisi records how people visited the Sphinx in order to ask for favours (fig. 51): 'A certain day of the year when visitors who aspire to senior jobs with the sultan offer incense to the Sphinx.'[46]

It is evident that there were elements of Egyptian mythology still present in early Islamic Egypt, but there were also numerous links between Egypt and Islam. Many key figures were married to Egyptian women, including Hajar, the Egyptian wife of Abraham, whose son Ismail was regarded as the Father of Arabs. Ismail and his father built the Kaaba, the most holy place in Islam and Egyptian craftsmen are recorded as being responsible for rebuilding it.[47] Even the Prophet Mohammed was married to an Egyptian woman, Maria, who was sent to him from Egypt with her sister, servants and gifts. The Prophet therefore regularly praised Egypt and there are a dozen or so *hadiths* (sayings of the Prophet) regarding Egypt, its produce and people.

Egypt was therefore key to the Islamic world, in the same way it was key to the Christian and Roman worlds (plate 11). This could be seen as a blessing or a curse, as during the latter years of the medieval period there were continuing invasions, beginning with the Christian crusades which started in 1095 CE,

51 The Sphinx at Giza

although it was not until the second wave in 1163 that Egypt was penetrated. The Egyptians defended their country from the onslaught by cutting the dykes, releasing the waters of the inundation and forcing the European invaders to retreat. This retreat was short lived. In 1164, Salah al-Din (Saladin) was forced to defend Egypt against the onslaught of the invading crusaders, who had reached as far as Middle Egypt. Although the Europeans once again left Egypt, they founded a residence in Al Qahira (Cairo) and a garrison at the gates to the city. The leader of the crusades at the time, Amalric, invaded Egypt a year later with an eye for settlement and the destruction was terrible. Fustat was razed to the ground, burning for nearly two months.[48] It was never to recover, and al-Qahira (Cairo) was to be the more prominent city:

> The city stretches over the banks of the Nile, river of paradise and receptacle of the rains of heaven, whose waters quench men's thirst and bring them abundance and wealth. I have walked its streets: they are thronged with crowds, and the markets are overflowing with every kind of merchandise.[49]

These markets were bustling noisy places, with animals and merchants milling around. By the eighteenth century Cairo was prospering so much that it was known as Umm al-Dunya, 'The mother of the World', and its population had doubled in just less than 200 years.

In 1218 the fifth wave of crusades focused their attentions on Egypt, entering through the Delta and laying siege to Damietta until it finally fell in 1219. However, the crusaders were still unfamiliar with the characteristics of the Nile and found themselves cut off by the rising waters, once again forced to evacuate Egypt, but only until 1249 and the next campaign. After defeating these crusading Europeans, Egypt was targeted by Genghis Khan and the Monguls, who were already successful in conquering China, Central Asia, Russia and much of Central Europe. Khan's brother, Hülegü, led the offensive on Cairo, instigated by a letter dispatched to the Egyptian ruler the Mamluk, Kutuz, outlining his intentions. Kutuz responded by killing the messengers, putting their heads on the gate at Bab Zuweila and leading an army to Palestine to meet the Monguls in 1260. The Mamluks were successful, winning Syria and protecting Egypt from further Mongul attacks.

Throughout these tough times there had been a series of low floods and from 1347 until 1834–35 Egypt also suffered greatly from the outbreaks of bubonic plague. Egypt was greatly depleted economically and in terms of population numbers. The arrival of the plague in 1347 was carefully documented:

> A ship arrived in Alexandria. Aboard it were thirty two merchants and a total of three hundred people – among them traders and slaves. Nearly all of them had died.

There was no one alive on the ship, save four of the traders, one slave, and about forty sailors. These survivors died in Alexandria.[50]

The plague killed a thousand people a day in Cairo and by 1349 a third of the entire population had died. There were to be nine outbreaks in the fifteenth century alone. This had a major effect on all aspects of Egyptian life, as the population was unable to adequately recover before another outbreak. Irrigation systems were neglected, falling into disrepair, and agriculture suffered because of it. In their weakened state, the trade relations also worsened as the Portuguese took over the ocean route along the coast of Africa to India, eventually dominating the Red Sea and Mediterranean, and it was only with the aid of the Ottomans that the Egyptian Mamluks were able win these trade routes back. This new ally was to charge heavily for their aid against the Portuguese, as Egypt was absorbed into the Ottoman Empire. Caliph Qaitbey (1468–1496 CE) tried to resist and constructed his fortress, in the 1480s (fig. 52), on the coast of Alexandria as the first line of defence, but it was too little too late and he was unsuccessful.

52 Qaitbey Fort, Alexandria. (*Courtesy of Brian Billington*)

Once again Egypt was governed remotely, this time from Istanbul, whilst the Egyptian Mamluk leaders maintained local control in Egypt as vassal rulers for the Turks. The crops of Egypt were now being sent to Istanbul, and they lost control of their foreign trading relationships. However, they were mostly left alone and were able to recover from the onslaught of plague, famines and warfare, with the population growing during this period from 3 million to 4.5 million. However, from 1760 to 1799 Egypt was once more suffering from the effects of the plague and there were internal conflicts between ruling Ottoman factions, which left Egypt open to foreign interest. This was to come in the form of Napoleon, who saw great potential in Egypt as a French colony.

🦌 10 🦌

A DONKEY RIDE AND
A BOATING TRIP
INTERSPERSED WITH RUINS

EIGHTEENTH AND NINETEENTH CENTURY

When Napoleon invaded Egypt and produced his *Description de L'Egypte*, the West was made aware of the splendours of Egypt – ancient and modern. This series of books were to be the first records of many sites in Egypt, despite the number of previous travellers. Napoleon landed in Alexandria on 1 July 1798 CE, taking up quarters initially near Pompey's Pillar.[1] The French saw Egypt as a way of expanding their empire through founding a French colony, and officially they claimed the occupation was to free the Egyptians from the Ottoman Empire,[2] marking Napoleon as a liberator.[3] He wanted to recreate and expand the empire of Alexander the Great, with himself as emperor. The French marched from Alexandria to Cairo through the desert where many hundreds of French soldiers, not used to the heat and hampered by their heavy clothes and equipment, died along the way. By the end of July that year, after the 'Battle of the Pyramids' (plate 12), the French army gained control of Lower Egypt,[4] losing only 29 men in the process.[5] This control, however, was not to last long.

Napoleon, like Alexander the Great, was accompanied by a large number of scholars, who were to provide Egypt with a modern infrastructure[6] and many were trained to build bridges, roads and canals – the basis of all civilisation. These scholars travelled with an entire library of books on Egypt and before leaving France they consulted numerous books, maps and papers.[7]

The English, however, were not prepared to allow France to create a colony, and Nelson confronted Napoleon, and was victorious against him in the Battle of the Nile in August 1798 at Abu Qir, near Alexandria. The French fleet sank and are beneath the sea to this day,[8] putting stay to Napoleon's dreams of being a modern Alexander the Great. After their defeat at Abu Qir, the French army was depleted and Napoleon left Egypt, sneaking out of Alexandria in October 1799, leaving his army[9] and scholars behind. He promised he would return the following May with reinforcements; however this was not to be the case and the army were abandoned.[10] Egypt was left under the authority of General Jean-Baptiste Kléber, who tried to maintain the French Colony, although the British demanded surrender.[11] He decided to fight and won a victory against the Turks at Heliopolis in 1800, but was assassinated by a Muslim fundamentalist later that year. He was succeeded by General 'Abdullah' Menou,[12] and it soon became apparent that Napoleon was planning to reinvade. The British attacked in March 1801, with General Abercromby and 18,000 men embarking on the coast of Egypt. The initial landing at Abu Qir saw 600 British casualties and the French driven from the beaches. The French eventually surrendered in June, whilst suffering from low morale and sickness, and readily agreed to leave Upper Egypt within 12 days.

All the while, Napoleon's scholars travelled from Alexandria to Philae in the south recording every place, monument or object of interest, and in the early days Napoleon partook in some of the visits. It is recorded that he spent time in the burial chamber of the Great Pyramid at Giza and apparently suffered an unusual experience, leaving him visibly shaken. He never spoke about it, and when later imprisoned in Saint Helena he seemed to be on the verge of discussing the experience only to dismiss it with 'you would never believe me anyway'. When the fruits of the labours of the French expedition were published as *Les Description*, between 1809 and 1828, it encouraged archaeologists, geologists, linguists and treasure hunters to travel to Egypt in their hoards.

The British escorted the French to Borg Rashid (Rosetta) to repatriate them, and closely examined their luggage before it was shipped. The French stated they would rather burn their notes and records than let the British have them, as this was to prove French intellectualism was greater than that of the British. They were therefore allowed to take their notes with them, including copies of inscriptions, images and maps, as well as a number of artefacts, starting a Europe-wide fashion for anything 'Nile-style'. One of the most significant artefacts was the zodiac ceiling from Denderah, currently housed in the Louvre in Paris.

However, when the expedition was at Rosetta, whilst demolishing an old wall, they uncovered a large stone (fig. 53). One of the artillery captains, Bouchard, realised it was covered in hieroglyphics and believed it may be valuable. He reported the stone to General Menou, who considered registering it as personal property but decided instead to transport it to Cairo and list it with the Institute.[13] The stone was confiscated by the British and was taken initially to the library of the Society of Antiquaries in London and then, in 1802, given as a gift to the British Museum.

Numerous copies of the text were made by the Institute in Cairo, using a combination of ink and graphite, as well as impressions using sulphur, which were sent to Paris. Further atrocities were inflicted upon the Rosetta Stone when it reached the Society of Antiquaries, where they made a series of plaster-casts of it, and then at the British Museum the inscription was whitened using chalk and the background covered in boot polish.[14] When the Museum, in recent years, cleaned the stone they discovered it was in fact dark grey with a red inscription rather than white as all the early representations show.

The Rosetta Stone is infamous as the key to the decipherment of hieroglyphs which were lost to the world in the sixth century CE, when Emperor Justinian closed the last Egyptian temple. Although the Rosetta Stone was the final key, for centuries scholars had been trying to decipher hieroglyphs. By the time the Rosetta Stone was discovered, two main assumptions about the language had been made: one, that hieroglyphics, hieratic and Demotic were connected, and, two, the system was phonetic. The Rosetta Stone confirmed these assumptions, as the text was written in three languages: hieroglyphics, Demotic and ancient Greek. Scholars were able to read Greek and matched the regular recognised Greek words, such as 'king' or 'god', with a similar number of occurrences in the Egyptian and Demotic. The text was the Memphis decree of Ptolemy V, written 27 March 196 BCE, and states a copy was to be erected in every temple in Egypt, which started a hunt for other bi- or tri- lingual stelae.

Four were discovered, one in Minuf (Delta), being used as a bench in front of a house, another near Tell el Yahudiyeh (Delta), which was used as an oil press, one at Naukratis, and the fourth at Elephantine, which is currently in the Louvre. Although there were multiple copies of this inscription bearing the same inscription, it is the Rosetta Stone that is infamous and iconic of the decipherment of hieroglyphs. The rivalry between the English and the French became clear in the race to unlock the meaning of hieroglyphs, with the main contenders being Thomas Young (1773–1829), an English physician, and Jean-François Champollion (1790–1832), a French philologist. Thomas Young made a major breakthrough with the recognition of the name of 'Ptolemy', enclosed in a cartouche,[15] and published his findings anonymously under the name ABCD, as he was concerned such unrelated research could affect his credentials as a physician. Although Young made the initial steps, he was unable to dedicate enough time to the problem and full decipherment was achieved three years later by Champollion.

In September 1822 Champollion was examining inscriptions from Abu Simbel and was able to read the names of Ramses and Thutmoses. Less than two weeks later he announced his success in the now infamous 'Letter to M. Dacier relating to the phonetic hieroglyphic alphabet used by the Egyptians'. In 1824 he published *A summary of the Hieroglyphic System of the Ancient Egyptians.* In August 1828 he travelled to Egypt for the first time to collect inscriptions and to correct records which were copied incorrectly, sailing along the Nile, first to Cairo and then as far as Abu Simbel at Aswan.[16] The expedition was partly financed by the

53 The Rosetta Stone. British Museum

Grand Duke of Tuscany and, other than Champollion, included 12 architects who all travelled by *dahibeya*.[17] Although he had an interest in the antiquities of Egypt and their conservation, Champollion was a man of his era and thought nothing of carving his name on temple walls (plate 13), or even cutting large blocks from the tomb walls of KV17, the tomb of Sety I in the Valley of the Kings, to take to France under the pretext of protecting them from flash floods. Champollion died in 1832 and his book on grammar was published posthumously by his brother.

The deciphering of hieroglyphs saw an increased interest in searching for antiquities, especially those with inscriptions. Even royalty participated in the hunt for relics and in 1672 CE King Louis XIV of France sent an expedition to Egypt in order to collect 'the greatest possible number of good manuscripts and ancient coins for His Majesty's library'.[18]

This trip awakened further interest in Egypt's antiquities, with people travelling to Egypt to study the monuments. The Jesuit priest Claude Sicard, in 1707 CE, visited Luxor and was the first European to reach Aswan. On his journey he saw 20 pyramids and 24 temples, and was to realise the importance of the Valley of the Kings at the discovery of 10 tombs, including KV2, created for Ramses IV. James Bruce, a Scotsman, further examined the Valley of the Kings in 1768 CE, and discovered the tomb of Ramses III, although it was already open and perhaps visited by Sicard.

The Franco-British rivalry was reawakened for the collection of the best relics, sometimes resulting in their destruction. Giovanni Battista Belzoni (1778–1824 CE), was working for the British collector Henry Salt, and was instrumental in some of the greatest discoveries in Egypt, including clearing the sand from Abu Simbel temple and discovering numerous tombs in the Valley of the Kings. The most impressive of these was that of Sety I, which contained the translucent calcite sarcophagus, minus its lid, which Henry Salt sold to Sir John Soames for £2000[19] – a considerable sum in the eighteenth century. Many items discovered by Belzoni were marked with his name, preventing other explorers claiming credit for discovering them (fig. 54). The large items, such as the statue of Ramses II from the Rammesseum, were dragged from their position in the temples and tombs to the river Nile where they could be taken to Cairo easily for eventual shipment to England.

Although hundreds of now famous Egyptologists and archaeologists were amongst these early visitors, anyone was able to excavate, and Belzoni even offered advice to rich amateurs as to where to dig in the Valley of the Kings. Tourists were looking for adventure, for something different to their own culture, and as this was the time of the French and British Empire, Europeans were looking to prove their Englishness or Frenchness, which was only achievable though visiting the 'exotic other' and comparing the natives' 'uncivilised' ways against their own 'civilised ones.'[20]

54 Belzoni carves his name on a statue of
Amenhotep III. British Museum

They were keen to witness as much unusual behaviour of the native Egyptians as possible as they travelled the Nile on a *dahibeya* (fig. 55) (a flat-bottomed house boat which could accommodate oars or a sail). The cabins were on the deck, with roofs forming an open-air drawing room. However, the comforts were limited and they could ether make or break the holiday. Although designed for the Nile and its currents, should there be crosswinds, the *dahibeya* needed to be towed by a steam boat. The average trip down the Nile took four or five months and the western tourists were accompanied by a dragoman, or guide, who aided all aspects of the journey and were invaluable to the independent traveller, although they were not trusted.

Schemes were devised by the Egyptians to get as much money from the tourists as possible, which did not prove to be that difficult. At the newly cleared site of Abu Simbel, for example, rather than keeping the doorway clear of sand, the locals deliberately allowed the sand to drift, charging exorbitant prices to clear it.[21] The dragoman was expected to keep his guest from such schemes, but was often at the centre of them. When ashore the travellers used donkeys, and a French traveller M. Ampère summed up a trip to Egypt as: 'A donkey ride and a boating trip interspersed with ruins.'

Although underwhelming as a description, it is an accurate one of a nine-teenth-century Nile trip. The standard journey started at Cairo, continuing down the Nile to Wadi Halfa, just below the second cataract, and was a slow and dangerous riverine journey with threats from currents, strong winds, crocodiles and the cataracts. Although many of the travellers visited some monuments, for the majority the ruins were simply part of the scenery to be enjoyed whilst moving. The captain generally allowed visitors to stop and explore when they were travelling downstream with the current, as the wind was too vital to miss on the upstream journey.[22]

The *dahibeya*s were expensive, and therefore travelling to Egypt in the early nineteenth century was limited to the very rich. As travel became popular, numerous travel guides were produced but the most popular was Murray's *Handbook for Travellers in Egypt*.[23] In 1843 the British Consul in Cairo complained of the 'flood' of tourists into Egypt, even though the numbers were minimal.[24] This was to increase ten-fold as, due to the increasing popularity of Egyptian travel, Thomas Cook and Sons decided to conduct tours to Egypt and the Holy Land. On the first Thomas Cook tour to Egypt in 1869 there were 32 bookings; they landed in Alexandria and travelled by train to Cairo (plate 14).[25] As visitors hated relying on dragomen, Thomas Cook eliminated this 'inconvenience' by dealing with all of the details himself. Gone were the days when there was a 'rude and clamorous' greeting at the Alexandrian dockyard. This was preserved only for those not travelling with Cook.[26]

Not only had the 'inconvenience' of the dragoman been removed, but also methods of transport were made more convenient. For the first trip in 1869, Cook hired two English-built steamers, the *Benha* and the *Beniswaif*, at £40 each. The steamers were far quicker than the *dahibeya*s, taking only 30 days to traverse the length of the Nile. An average trip required two days in Alexandria, 14 days in Cairo, 21–24 days on the Nile to Aswan, with three or four days' stop in Luxor.[27] This was a vast difference to the four or five months of the *dahibeya* journey.

Onboard there was a daily routine of coffee at 8 a.m., breakfast at 10 a.m., lunch at 1 p.m., dinner at 6.30 p.m. and tea at 8 p.m.: the first all-inclusive package tour. The boats, however, were not clean, and the passengers suffered from what Cook called F sharps (fleas) but not B flats (bugs).[28] Murray, in his guide *Handbook for travellers to Egypt*, stated that the steamers 'should be sunk before a voyage to rid them of rats' and 'other noxious inhabitants'.[29] To solve these problems, in 1869 Thomas Cook hired a new steamer, the *Beherah*, which carried 44 tourists. When Murray returned to Cairo at the end of the trip in 1870, he was appointed agent for Nile Passenger Traffic, hiring the Khedive's steamers which he refurbished. Cook controlled all passenger steam-boat traffic on the Nile as far as the first and second cataracts,[30] enabling the company to work to a profit. In 1885–86, when John Mason Cook ran the company, they built a new Nile fleet of their own:

'The new steamers will be floating palaces and will be finer than anything that has floated on the grand old river since the days of Cleopatra. They will cause a sensation and I hope will prove a great attraction.'[31]

These would, therefore, be a far cry from the rat and flee-infested steamers employed for the first trip to Egypt (fig. 56). These steamers were also a topic of conversation for the independent traveller, where the conduct of the tourists and the vessels were criticised. Pierre Loti in 1910 laments:

> Poor Luxor! Along the banks is a row of tourist boats, a sort of two or three storeyed [sic] barracks, which nowadays infest the Nile from Cairo to the Cataracts. Their whistlings and the vibration of their dynamos make an intolerable noise. How shall I find a quiet place for my *dahibeya*, where the functionaries of Messrs Cook will not come to disturb me.[32]

55 A *Dahibeya* on the Nile. (*Reproduced with permission of the Griffith Institute, University of Oxford*)

Despite the condition of the original boats and the hostility of the independent travellers, the first journey was an exciting one as for most of the trip the *Benha* and *Beniswaif* were sailing behind Edward, the Prince of Wales. The royal party, however, were a couple of days ahead, in a fleet of six blue and gold steamers each towing a barge of necessities and luxuries which included 3000 bottles of champagne and 4000 of claret. The prince had also brought his own taxidermist to stuff any animals hunted whilst on the trip.[33] Even Miss Riggs, one of Thomas Cook's first customers to Egypt, packed her riding saddle[34] as Thomas Cook and Sons actively encouraged hunting and it was possible to purchase a licence and the ammunition with which to shoot quail from them.[35] One traveller records killing 10,000 birds in one season[36] – a boast worthy of the pharaohs.

However, simple Nile cruises were not enough for Thomas Cook and it had long been his ambition to travel 'to Egypt via China', which became possible at the end of 1869 following the opening of the Suez Canal. The Suez Canal was the result of Napoleon's invasion of Egypt in 1798, when his savants discovered the ruins of the Necho's canal connecting the Red Sea and Nile. When Napoleon returned to Paris he discussed resurrecting this waterway but between the Mediterranean and the Red Sea, which was a fundamental factor in his Egyptian campaigns, as it would allow French ships clear access to the eastern markets.[37] Britain had turned down the offer of shares in the Suez Canal and subsequently snubbed the opening, but ironically they benefited most from the speedier routes the canal offered.

Thomas Cook organised a trip for the opening of the canal on 17 November 1869. He had difficulties recruiting for it and in the end only 30 people booked. There were two ceremonies watched by international dignitaries in Port Said: one for Roman Catholic France and one for Muslim Egypt. There were no British dignitaries at the opening ceremonies other than an untitled representative from the foreign office. Empress Eugenie of France travelled aboard the *L'Aigle* with Emperor Francis Joseph of Austria, the first of 67 ships making the historic journey from the Mediterranean to the Red Sea. Behind were yachts with Khedive Ismail, the Prince Royal of Prussia, Prince Henry of the Netherlands, and 36th in line was Thomas Cook on a paddle steamer, *America*,[38] which had been refurbished as a hotel. The dignitaries were greeted by a gun salute, which was overshadowed when the firework store accidently blew up 'very nearly demolishing the town'.[39] After the opening ceremonies Cook and his party travelled by rail to Cairo to attend a meal hosted by the khedive.

After its opening and due to the extravagance of Khedive Ismail, he was forced to sell his shares of the Suez Canal. Britain, with a loan of £4 million from Rothschild's Bank, purchased them, making them controlling shareholders. Until this the French were the controlling foreigner in North Africa. This eventually led to the British occupation of Egypt. The Egyptian economy was so tied in with

56 Aboard a Nile
Steamer. (*Courtesy
of the Thomas Cook
Archives*)

the British and French that the revenue of the Suez Company was put under
European management. Half of Egypt's revenue paid their public debt and Lord
Cromer (Captain Evelyn Baring) was sent to Cairo as British Commissioner of
the Debt, causing public anger against foreign occupation.[40]

By the time of the opening of the Suez Canal, tourism in Cairo had expanded
enough to warrant the building of large hotels. Thomas Cook and Sons' tours stayed
at the newly built Shepheard's Hotel near Cairo's Ezbekiyah Square. The square was
open park land, with lush greenery and rare trees, and the land had was purchased from
Abbas Pasha for the price of two whippets called Bess and Ben.[41] Samuel Shepheard
managed the hotel from 1841, and in 1845 the hotel was renamed after him.

Initially the hotel was not well favoured and was described by Mark Twain
(1835–1910) as the second worst hotel on earth; by Edward Lear (1812–1888) as 'a
pig-sty mixed with a bear-garden'; and by John Gardiner Wilkinson (1797–1875),
who was slightly more subtle, who stated the food 'leaves a lot to be desired'.
Murray, in his *Handbook*, said it was still better than the steamers. Shepheard took
these comments to heart, making improvements in 1870 just after the Suez opening, adding marble columns, chandeliers, elaborate carpets and muted lighting,
and it slowly became the place to see and be seen at the end of the nineteenth
century, with meetings over tea often held on the terrace:

Costumes of every kind, complexions of every shade, and tongues of every nation, greet the eye and salute the ear: dragomans settling accounts with victimised tourists, vendors of photographs, shawls and jewellery, offering their wares; now one's attention is distracted by a juggler, who with carpet spread, is 'thimble rigging', and drawing long strings of medals out of his throat, before he finishes his conjuring tricks; another arrives with trained monkeys, dog and goat, and solicits our attention to his exhibition; scarcely have we time to look at him when an Egyptian serpent charmer comes, and shows with what familiarity he can handle reptiles and make them into neckties … And thus the time speeds on to 6:30 pm, when the sound of the dinner gong disperses the artistes, and calls the visitors to the *table d'hôte*, and darkness and silence fall upon the city.[42]

Shepheard's was clearly a lively place to visit – a real hub of activity. In this year Thomas Cook and Sons took advantage of this and established an office within the grounds of the hotel,[43] increasing visitor numbers. Amelia Edwards describes some of the characters who travelled here:

Here are invalids in search of health; artists in search of subjects; sportsmen keen upon crocodiles; statesmen out for holiday; special correspondents alert for gossip: collectors on the scent of papyri and mummies; men of science with only scientific ends in view; and the usual surplus of idlers who travel for the mere love of travel, or the satisfaction of a purposeful curiosity.[44]

One of the most important aspects of the tourist trade in the late nineteenth century was the health resort. From the end of the eighteenth century, the weather in Egypt was considered more clement than Europe and poor heath brought hundreds of people here. There were six health resorts throughout Egypt, at Alexandria, Cairo, Mena House at Giza, Helwan, Luxor and Aswan. Each offered something different: Alexandria, sea breezes, with a drier and warmer climate, especially at night, than Cairo. Cairo, on the other hand, was more popular, with many staying at the Mena House at Giza which at the time was 8km from the city. This palace had been turned into a hotel by Mr Locke-King and although balconies were, in the 1880s, unheard of in hotels, it was decided every room should have one overlooking the pyramids, and as the air was cleaner, drier and fresher than in Cairo it was a popular choice. Only 16 miles south of Cairo were the Sulphur and Salt Springs of Helwan, believed to have healing properties. As its popularity increased, baths were built here for tourists suffering from skin complaints.

The south, however, was the most desirable place to go for recuperation, as it had less wind than the north and had constant sunshine and warmth, which is 'extremely grateful to delicate folk'.[45] This resort originated with John Mason

Cook, who opened the Luxor Hotel in 1878 as a sanatorium for pulmonary diseases. It was thought the invalids would benefit from the dry air and there was a doctor available on site for emergencies. For the second season a new wing was added, doubling the capacity to 45 bedrooms.[46] Initially it did not receive positive reviews and Murray went as far as to say the accommodation was 'not good', the food was poor 'and unsuited to invalids' and, at 15s a day, was expensive. In 1886 the Winter Palace Hotel was built to cope with the increased number of tourists to the region and was competition for the Luxor Hotel:

> The thing which dominates the whole town, and may be seen five or six miles away, is the Winter Palace, a hasty modern production which has grown on the border of the Nile during the past year; a colossal hotel, obviously sham, made of plaster and mud, on a framework of iron. Twice or three times as high as the admirable Pharaonic temple, its impudent facade rises there, painted a dirty yellow.[47]

The Winter Palace became an important hotel for the rich and influential, and it was on the notice board here that Howard Carter announced the discovery of the tomb of Tutankhamun to the world. He stayed at the hotel regularly, even though he had accommodation on the west bank, and was often seen in the gardens having tea, until his death in the 1960s.

Further south, in Aswan, the weather was even drier with warm evenings, and was considered even more beneficial. Many hotels were built here, including the Cataract Hotel, in 1900, built by Thomas Cook to cater for his own tourists (fig. 57). The first advertisement, in 1899, in *The Egyptian Gazette* emphasised: 'Every modern comfort. Large and small apartment rooms, library, billiard room etc. … fireplaces in hall, salons and the main rooms. Electrical lights running all night. Perfect sanitary arrangements approved by the authorities. Can accommodate 60 visitors.'

Its value as a health resort was emphasised by W.E. Kingsford in his book *Assouan as a Health Resort* (1900):

> In the construction of this hotel, great attention has been given to the requirements of the invalids – most of the rooms have verandas, and a warm, sunny aspect; many are fitted with fireplaces, and the position and form of the building has been chosen to provide shelter from the prevailing winds.
>
> Every modern convenience is provided for in the form of electric light, hot and cold baths, &c., and a … number of private sitting rooms to meet the requirements of invalids.
>
> There is an English Physician and nurse in Assouan, and an English house-keeper is in charge of the domestic arrangements of the Hotel.[48]

57 The Cataract Hotel, Aswan. (*Courtesy of the Thomas Cook Archives*)

It is clear the Cataract Hotel was very modern, with up-to-date commodities reaching not only European but English standards. In 1900 the hotel was enlarged and was described in *The Telegraph* as 'unmatched even in Europe'. Its popularity grew and, in 1901, tents were needed in the grounds to accommodate overflowing demand.

This increased tourism was not viewed favourably by all and there was a great deal of snobbery regarding package tourists. William Howard Russell, a journalist, comments on this new type of tourism:

> That is a nuisance to the ordinary traveller to have his peace broken, to have a flood of people poured into a quiet town, to have hotels and steamers crammed, to see his pet mountain peak crested with bonnets and wideawakes, to behold his favourite valley filled up with a flood of 'mere English, whom no one knows.' I am not prepared to deny; but what are we to say to 'the greatest good of the greatest number?' Let us reflect and submit. The people at Alexandria were, as far as I could judge, very respectable – it was only in the concrete they became disagreeable. Mr Monpensier Brown and Miss Clara de Mowbray may be the capital companions as individuals, in the abstract but as 'Cook's Tourists' they become an aggregate of terrors.[49]

Amelia Edwards comments in 1873 that a visitor 'distinguishes at first sight between a Cook's tourist and an independent traveller'. Captain John Ardagh went on to comment 'We had four seasons, which we distinguished as follows: first, flies; second, mosquitoes; third, flying bugs; fourth, Cook's Tourists.' There is very little that is essentially different between these early tourists and modern tourists. There are still two types of travellers: the independent traveller and the package tourist, and each will have a personal agenda in travelling to Egypt. Some will be in Egypt as students or scholars, wanting to learn, others for a relaxing break in a beautiful environment, and for many it is for the 'checklist' to say they have visited the pyramids and Tutankhamun's tomb. The big differences lie in the nature of tourism in the modern world, which is quick and easy and available to all. This can be accredited to Thomas Cook and Sons who introduced the first package tours; they were not the only ones in the late nineteenth century but they were certainly the first.

However, tourism was different as tourists were openly encouraged to hunt for antiquities, whereas today a decent tour guide should stop their guests from touching, sitting and standing on the monuments. Nonetheless, in the nineteenth century they 'were advised to take candles for tombs, a fine sieve for sifting out those shards, and some small excavating tools'.[50]

Any antiquities discovered were taken to the Cairo Museum to assess their value before allowing them to leave the country. All that was needed for this exportation to happen was an officially stamped document,[51] which was easy to come by.

The hunt for antiquities brings us full circle to the beginning of the chapter and the start of travel as a means of collecting. It is clear the development of tourism in Egypt was the result of the Franco-British rivalry, instigated by imperialism and the desire to occupy Egypt to protect access to Indian and Chinese trade routes. Initially Napoleon and Nelson were fighting over the land; then the race to decipher hieroglyphs was between Young and Champollion, an Englishman and a Frenchman; and then there developed an international hunt for 'treasure' and antiquities which started with the Belzoni/Drovetti competition for bringing antiquities back to Europe and then between the Louvre and the British Museum for possession of them. This rivalry, however, has been invaluable to Egyptology as a discipline, and one wonders whether the *Description* would have been written if Napoleon had won the battle at Abu Qir. Without this, Europe would be largely unaware of the wonders Egypt had to offer, and there is always the possibility that the Rosetta Stone would never have been found. The rivalry, therefore, has been instrumental to the basis of Egyptology and modern travel to Egypt as well as the founding of two of the greatest Egyptology collections in the world: the Louvre and the British Museum.

11

PROSPERITY AND WATER GO HAND IN HAND

EIGHTEENTH TO TWENTIETH CENTURY

At the same time as the travel industry was booming, Egypt was going through a number of improvements and innovations in technologies, in water management in particular. The instigator of many of these new commercial schemes was the Turkish Pasha, Mohammed Ali (fig. 58).

The early years of Pasha Mohammed Ali's reign were difficult due to the poorly managed economy of Egypt. One of the first changes to be introduced was a re-organisation of the army, with a totally new military regime, but the Mamluks protested against it. Mohammed Ali was tired of retaliation and invited 500 Mamluk amirs to a celebration at the citadel in 1811. As they were about to leave, the doors were locked and they were slaughtered by Albanian mercenaries. A further 1000 Mamluks were hunted and killed in the streets of Cairo; any survivors fled south where they were either killed by Mohammed's son Ibrahim or were exiled in Nubia, leaving Egypt in the hands of Mohammed Ali.[1] Mohammed Ali, during his time in Egypt, brought the Ottoman Empire to the brink of collapse, which the British wanted to prevent. Although British relations with the Ottomans were deteriorating, they relied heavily on Egyptian shipments and believed the only answer was occupation, in order to protect their grain supply, trade to India and ultimately to prevent the French from occupying Egypt. The British fleet anchored at Alexandria in 1882, forcing Mohammed Ali's troops to withdraw from Crete, Syria, Arabia and Yemen, annexing them in Egypt. This saw the start of the British occupation.

During the early years of Pasha Mohammed Ali, the army was maintained by a system of conscription of Egyptian peasants. To avoid this, many people resorted to self-mutilation by damaging one of their eyes. Mohammed resolved this by having a regiment of one-eyed men. Initially the officers were Europeans, but military training schools for Egyptians were founded. A number of technical, surveying (1816) and medical (1827) schools were set up, with the medical schools initiating a vaccination programme in 1819 against smallpox. Every year smallpox killed 50,000 children, and outbreaks of plagues such as the bubonic plague in 1834–1835 killed a further third of the population of Cairo.

Mohammed Ali reformed Egypt into a modern industrial society using European techniques and models, and hiring Europeans for factory management, civil engineering, military training and medicine. Many European visitors to Egypt were interviewed by him personally as he tried to gain as much information as possible. From this research and interviews, in 1837 he set up a centralised bureaucracy, with district and local organisations rationalised with clear lines of authority. He reluctantly introduced a train line between Alexandria and Cairo, which was continued by his grandson Ismail after his death, and ran the full length of the Egyptian Nile. Until this point the cataract area at Aswan alone took 2–3 days to navigate and was highly dangerous at low water, taking 50–100 men to drag and pole the boat past the rapids. The train eradicated this obstacle, making Nile travel easier and quicker.

58 Mohammed Ali. (*Courtesy of Photos.com*)

More importantly, Mohammed Ali instigated a programme of irrigation and agriculture, improving Egypt's natural resources and exportation capabilities. The most lucrative introduction was the planting of cotton to sell to Europe. To ensure its success, he banned imports of cheap British cotton which could compete with the Egyptian.[2] As cotton requires water in the late spring and summer, at a time when the Nile was low, it required extensive artificial irrigation. Thus Egyptians were conscripted to dig and maintain earthworks (i.e. canals and dykes) or to protect river banks during the inundation.[3] In 1816, Mohammed Ali used the corvée system to dig new irrigation canals, and between 1817 and 1820 conscripted 300,000 workers, of which 100,000 died – 20,000 whilst building the Mahmudiya Canal.

His impatience led to numerous schemes being started at once, and he is accredited with 32 canals, 10 dykes, 41 dams and barrages. He also reclaimed thousands of acres of agricultural land from the desert,[4] bringing it into cultivation and increasing the crops from one a year to three.[5] In order to build these structures Mohammed Ali used the monuments of ancient Egypt as quarries, as he regarded them simply as natural resources to be used for construction, or as political tools and gifts for eminent visitors. During his rule there was no museum for antiquities and no legislation on their removal, as such many important pieces left the country during this period.[6]

At the start of Mohammed's rule, Egypt's finances had been mismanaged for years. Initially he confiscated the estates of the Mamluks and endowments of religious guilds, who owned a fifth of Egypt's agricultural land. Now all land was state owned. He introduced a series of taxes, calculations based on the height of the inundation, which kick-started when the Nile rose to a sixteenth of a cubit. Depending on when it reached this height they were able to calculate whether there would be a high or low flood and charge taxes accordingly.[7] In addition to these, there were other taxes, including 'the good news tax' and the 'solidarity tax.' The latter meant if one farmer was unable to pay his taxes, the farmer next door would be expected to pay in addition to his own. This continued from village to village.[8]

The pasha looked to the West for innovation on how to increase agricultural land, in particular machinery which could help with his irrigation programme. It was this that led Giovanni Battista Belzoni (1778–1823 CE) to Egypt with the hope of selling his design for a new water-lifting device.[9] In Italy, Belzoni was a circus strong man due to his height (6ft 7in) and strength. Whilst travelling back to England after entertaining Wellington's troops he met an agent of Mohammed Ali, who had expressed an interest in his machine.[10]

He travelled to Egypt in 1815 with the intention of first meeting the English Consul Ernest Misset and the French Consul Bernardino Drovetti, both of whom could be invaluable in introducing him to the right people. In one letter to Drovetti, Belzoni explained the benefits of his new machine:

I have made various surveys of the land near the Nile, observing that an enormous quantity is wasted for lack of water as it is not flooded by the Nile. In consideration of the ease with which they could be irrigated, particularly when the Nile is high, it would be extremely useful to succeed in this endeavour.[11]

He was aware that the British had given a hydraulic machine to the pasha, but it was viewed as ineffective as it had not flooded the fields immediately and was abandoned in the gardens at Subra Palace. Belzoni believed his machine could operate better and presented the idea to the pasha. Whilst he was building the prototype, Mohammed Ali insisted Belzoni, his wife Sarah and their servant James Curtain stayed in the palace grounds.[12] The machine was rather like a crane, with a wheel and a drum, into which an ox was placed. The steps of the ox moved the drum, pulling buckets of water from the river to the fields. The demonstration showed the machine could move seven times more water than the waterwheels currently used. The pasha was satisfied but his officials were not, although they could not articulate why. As a form of amusement, perhaps to lighten the atmosphere, the pasha ordered 15 farmers to step into the drum to compare their output against that of the ox. Belzoni's servant joined the farmer, but once the machine started they were frightened and jumped out into the river. Curtain, in the confusion, was knocked to the ground and broke his thigh. This was viewed as a bad omen by the pasha and his men, and the project was rejected.[13]

This was, however, an excuse, as there was a general mistrust of machinery which could put numerous men and oxen out of work. Belzoni discovered oxen were raised solely for operating waterwheels and by eliminating them from this task would deprive the farmers of a large majority of their incomes. Whilst Belzoni had been waiting for approval from the pasha, the English Consul had been replaced by Henry Salt. Belzoni was introduced to him and agreed to work for him in discovering and removing antiquities; a lucrative business for both.[14]

Although this setback caused Belzoni to change his career, Mohammed Ali continued in his quest to irrigate more land. It became clear that canals and ditches were not enough and he started investigating other avenues of water management, beginning with a campaign of building barrages diverting water to the places requiring it.[15] This was incorporated into the religion and there was a ceremony referred to as the 'Cutting of the Dam' in Cairo, which began the day after the tax announcements. Each year a dam was built at the mouth of the Khalig Canal and, a short distance from the dam, a mound of earth called the 'bride', representative of a virgin, was sacrificed to the Nile.[16] Once the inundation receded the dam was thinned out until it was destroyed by a boat sailing into it. This ceremony was often accompanied by singing, dancing and fireworks,[17] celebrating the start of the agricultural calendar and the fertilisation of the land.

Napoleon had introduced the practice of regulating water flow, forcing it down the Rosetta and the Damietta branches and so doubling the effect of the annual flood. This was continued by Mohammed Ali in 1833, when he built a stone dam at the head of the Rosetta branch, diverting the water to the Damietta branch and providing the water supply for the Delta. The chief engineer of public works and the chief engineer of the Suez Canal were concerned about the effect this would have on Alexandria and the eastern Delta, and appealed to Mohammed Ali, who capitulated and built a barrage across the head of each branch in 1833–1835 until the work ground to a halt.

In 1842 Mougel Bey, a French Engineer, suggested a series of barrages would unite a series of fortresses in the Delta and solve the problems with the water supply throughout the Delta. The Damietta barrage was started in 1843 and the Rosetta barrage in 1847, which were finished in 1861, although they were not built well. The Rosetta barrage had 61 arches and two locks, and was 460m long; the Damietta barrage had 61 arches and two locks and was 527m long. In 1863 the Rosetta barrage gates were closed to divert water to the Damietta branch but large cracks appeared in the structure and the 10 arches moved out of place because the floor was cracked and the foundations were too shallow. Parts of the structure had not been finished and the Damietta barrage had not been fitted with gates. Mougel was blamed for this initial failure even though it was the haste and impatience of Mohammed Ali that was the problem.[18] Despite money pumped into the series of Delta barrages, they still did not hold enough water to irrigate the cotton and other crops during the summer. Although by the end of the nineteenth century numerous barrages, dams and dykes raised the water level, channelling it to the fields, there was no capability of storing water from one year to the next.[19] This was to be the emphasis of water management in the twentieth century.

At the death of Mohammed Ali, his grandson Abbas Hilmy I (1813–1854), took over as pasha, but greatly neglected many of Mohammed's schemes due to being anti-Western, refusing to incorporate European ideas and technologies. Many of the schools and factories were closed, and the army was reduced. Despite this, he eventually realised the importance of introducing the Alexandria to Cairo railway, which was completed in 1856, with a railway between Cairo and Suez following shortly after; both were to be beneficial to Egypt. However, Abbas was never able to pull Egypt out of debt and the Crimean War only made it worse. Said (1822–1863), the successor of Abbas, died owing over £7 million, leaving a broken country to his successor Ismail. However, the most ambitious scheme of Said was the construction of the Suez Canal which shortened the sailing time between Europe and the East. The 170km of land between the Red Sea and the Mediterranean was flat, and the canal construction simply required digging a ditch. The scheme was proposed by Ferdinand de Lesseps, the French Consul, during the reign of Mohammed Ali and

Said agreed to it, with the concession that he would personally hold 15 per cent and Egypt another 15 per cent of the shares of the Suez Canal Company. Said purchased further shares until he held 44 per cent. The £6 million required to build the canal was partially raised through the sale of the remaining shares and Said made up the difference by providing the manpower through the corvée. This came to a total of 20,000 men a month and just as many died due to malnutrition, neglect, overwork or accidents, an amount that formed nearly 5 per cent of the total population. This caused a major economic backlash.[20] Said died in 1863, to be succeeded by Ismail (1863–1879) who continued the building programme and improving the irrigation systems due to the increased European demand for Egyptian products.

He continued the construction of the Suez Canal, completing the Sweet Water Canal, from the eastern desert to the Suez Canal, providing clean drinking water, harbours and two important towns: Ismailia and Port Said. However, there were international concerns regarding the corvée, viewed as little less than slave labour, and in 1864 once again the construction on the Suez Canal was stopped, until 1869 when work was resumed and completed the same year. The opening ceremonies were an ideal opportunity for Ismail to show Europe how cultured and technological the Egyptians were. However, £11.5 million had been spent by Egypt on the canal and the Suez Canal Company did not start making a profit until 1875, with negotiable amounts staying in Egypt.

Nonetheless, Ismail's extravagance and poor financial management pushed Egypt into further debt, until it finally fell into European hands. Initially, when he came into power, Ismail concentrated on building elaborate palaces, destroying hundreds of homes in the process. He tried to improve the natural resources and efficiency of Egypt by building more bridges, canals, railroads and introducing a good postal service via steam boats along the Nile. He reopened a number of the educational institutions shut down by Abbas, emphasising their importance and by the end of his reign literacy had risen by 5 per cent.

In addition to the irrigation programmes, Ismail took an interest in the resource market, adjusting his programme to counteract it, so when the cotton prices slumped he cut the Ibrahamieh Canal from Assyut to the Delta, introducing sugar cane[21] which is still one of the most important crops in Egypt, and sadly one that causes the most damage to the ancient monuments (see Epilogue). The income from cotton halved in the 1860s, affecting the tax revenue and resulting in bankruptcies and closure of many countryside businesses. Ismail retaliated by increasing taxes and then ultimately selling future tax revenues in 1871 by encouraging landowners to pay six times the tax so in future they would only pay half.[22] In 1875 Ismail sold his shares in the Suez Canal Company to Britain and stopped making payments on their international debt amounting to £100 million, ten times the Egyptian annual budget.

English and French representatives came to Egypt to manage the debt, and by 1879 Ismail had been deposed by his son Tewfiq (1852–1892). It was not long before he had given control of Egypt to the British. The British did not only occupy Egypt but also the Sudan, consequently dominating the entire Nile basin.

Throughout the reign of Khedive Ismail, the Nile reached its capacity, as it could only support 7 million people and the population had risen to 7.8 million in 1882.[23] The need for water and increased agricultural land was desperate, and a programme of dams and barrages was begun in the Delta, with a barrage across the Damietta and Rosetta branches of the Nile. By 1890 the Delta barrage could hold 13ft of water and the British began plans for storage of surplus flood water in the summer; the beginning of the first Aswan dam,[24] which was begun in 1898 at the first cataract, holding water to a level of 106m above sea level. The dam affected the local environment and many villagers were re-housed in 'luxurious' accommodation with air conditioning, piped water, electric lighting and deliveries of ice from an ice plant.[25] When the dam was completed a lake was constructed behind it[26] which totally submerged the nearby temple of Philae. Enough water would be released from the dam to water the maize crops from the end of July to October, during the inundation. By October the winter cereals, beans and berseem only required limited water, so less was released, and in late February further water was released from the dam, keeping the cotton and rice watered. In this way the agricultural land of Egypt was always kept at optimum water levels.

Not long after the dam was built, due to the continuing population growth, there were plans to heighten it. In 1907 Sir Benjamin Baker, an engineer, suggested heightening the dam could be carried out by welding new masonry to the top of the old. This was carried out and completed in 1912, and was raised yet again in 1933, and at this point it held 1.5 cubic miles of water. By the reign of King Farouk (1936–1965) a further 800,000 crop acres had been reclaimed and the population had grown by a further 5 million people. Every acre supported seven people and was stretched to capacity. The Aswan dam no longer produced enough water, which had led to studies by British hydrologists and engineers of Nile flow and resulted in the Nile Waters Agreement of 1929, enabling the Egyptians to improve and control the waters of the Nile whilst still allotting enough water to the Sudan for their needs.[27] After much discussion, the idea for the High Dam at Aswan was proposed and accepted. The Egyptians hoped the dam would provide extra security by giving them control over the river, as for centuries they were concerned about their dependence on the river and how they could be destroyed should anyone interfere with the source.[28] However, one of the limitations of the dam was its vulnerability. Although it allowed Egypt control over the water, should there be any fault in the dam or should an atomic bomb be dropped near it, the results would be disastrous, leaving only those in the Oasis, in canal zones or those who escaped to the desert in safety.[29]

Once the idea for the High Dam had been accepted it took many years for it to materialise, mainly due to funding, politics and problems identifying the correct materials and technology. Other implications to the building of the dam included the construction of approach routes, a small industrial town with factories and workshops built in the remote desert with a limited water supply, as well as the destruction of entire villages in the vicinity:

> In the years to come, those who travel by boat from the Dam into the Sudan will travel through an empty world, with the mud-built villages dissolved beneath them, palm trees rotting deep in the water, and a few solid buildings like the hotel at Wadi Halfa lying well below their keels as ghostly havens for Nubian fish.[30]

The High Dam was built in the reservoir of the original dam, which was absorbed into the newly created Lake Nasser. The dam was built across the Nile between two valleys, (Khor Agama and Khor Khundi) where the banks rise 33m above the river. The base of the river was reinforced by driving hollow drills into the river bed, through sand, silt, debris and granite, until hitting bedrock; these holes were then filled with a combination of 80 per cent Aswan clay and 20 per cent concrete.[31] The first part of the construction project was to build a coffer dam, and there was a public ceremony for the destruction of the starter blocks, with more trucks of rubble on display than were needed in order to make a big show. Nasser and Krushchev of the Soviet Union pressed the button to destroy the blocks that opened the sluices, diverting the river. Not long after the river was diverted, the greatest flood of the century was reported to be travelling down the Blue Nile.

The floods between 1961 and 1964 comprised the amount of water it had been estimated would take decades to produce. The Russian engineers wanted all the gates on the dam to remain open so as not to put any undue pressure on the coffer dams, with the reasoning that land would grow again and village houses could be rebuilt. The surplus water flowed past Aswan washing away maize, sugar and vegetables, destroying villages and crops, and causing loss of life from Aswan to Cairo. By September the Delta towns were evacuated and the floods still showed no sign of abating, so the Russians closed two of the tunnels and partially closed a third, limiting the amount of water flowing through.[32]

Although the High Dam's construction began in 1952 it was not completed until 1970. It was 978m at the base and 41m wide at the top, running 3,657m long, containing the same amount of building material as 17 Great Pyramids.[33] The dam produced a series of positive and negative effects, changing many aspects of Egyptian culture and travel. In the 18 years it took to build the dam the population had grown to such an extent that they consumed the products produced by the newly cultivated land immediately. Rather than solving all the poverty problems as was planned, it simply bought time so Egypt would not get any poorer. People reacted to the High Dam in different ways: some believed it would endanger Egypt rather than help it, and others believed it to be a grandiose project which masked rather than addressed the political problems.

The measurable effects included the fact that the coffer dam blocked the Nile and halted the steamer service between Egypt and the Sudan, which had been used by tourists for a century. The environmental effects included decreased fertility in surrounding agricultural lands, serious erosion downstream, an inundation of the Delta with seawater and a decrease in the fish populations of the Mediterranean.[34] A lake has formed in the field near Gisr el Bahlawan in the Fayum which is a shocking pink colour due to the high saline content. The landowners have to import sand to dump onto the fields to raise them above this stagnant water and to try to reverse the infertility caused by the salinated water.[35] The local climate in Aswan has also changed since Lake Nasser was built, as cumulous (storm) clouds form on most days, resulting in light rain every four years. The stones in the Aswan region will not survive well in a wet environment as granite and feldspar decompose quickly. This means, for example, that the unfinished obelisk in the Aswan quarry could vanish forever.[36]

The building of the Aswan High Dam and the subsequent flooding of Lake Nasser, which extends for 300 miles from Aswan to the Dal Cataract in the Sudan, not only drowned many Sudanese villages but also threatened a series of ancient temples, tombs and monuments, many of which still languish beneath the water, lost forever. However, it was decided that some of the monuments should be saved and a committee was formed to choose which these would be. Initially in May 1964, as a means of using the excess rock removed for the creation of the dam and of protecting the temples, a small coffer dam was built around them. However, this was not enough and further plans were made.

Of the hundreds of monuments threatened, only a few were earmarked for rescue. Britain offered to move two Buhen temples for £8000, Holland offered £120,000 to move the Semna East temple, the Serra West temple and the tomb of Djehutyhotep, which are all in Khartoum. The others were simply recorded in as much detail as possible before they were lost forever. Abu Simbel, Philae and Kalabsha temples were moved to higher ground and some temples were moved abroad, including the Ptolemaic temple of Debod, currently in Madrid (plate 15), the temple of Dendur now in New York, the Graeco-Roman temple of Taffa now in Leiden and the temple of al-Lessiya in Turin.[37]

The temple of Kalabsha was second in size to Abu Simbel and was built by the Roman emperor Augustus using reused blocks from a New Kingdom temple on the same site. Even before the High Dam was constructed Kalabsha was of some interest as the original dam at Aswan caused it to flood annually, so it was possible to sail through the temple.[38] Alexandre Barsanti was in control of the conservation of the temple in 1907–09, although the danger to the temple was far worse than he imagined as the foundations were on alluvium and not bedrock. As the foundations became saturated with water the temple was at risk of collapse. The concerns of these early conservationists were aesthetics to make the temple more appealing to tourists. Barsanti caused more damage than he prevented by filling the holes in the masonry with cement, preventing the drainage of water when the floods abated each year.[39]

With the building of the High Dam, Kalabsha was earmarked to be moved north of its original location, to higher ground on the west bank.[40] In August 1961 the contract was signed and work began dismantling the temple. At this time the temple was still partially submerged, so the initial recording and dismantling began when it was under water. Only one course of masonry a day was removed as the waters abated. To reach the uppermost courses of the temple walls row boats were used and scaffolding and cranes mounted on pontoons. The blocks were loaded onto Nile barges before being taken ashore. Each of the blocks was marked and numbered so they could be reconstructed accurately before being moved into temporary storage. The blocks were colour coded so they would be easily distinguished, with blue for the pylon blocks and yellow for the Hypostyle Hall, for example. The store built to house the blocks covered an area of 25–30,000 square metres, 15 times bigger than the temple itself.[41] After three years of recording, cutting and removing 13,000 blocks, it was re-erected in 1970, complete with 30m of causeway in front of the main entrance.[42] When the project was begun the temple was in very poor condition with no roofing blocks in place, and the pylon appeared unfinished. These issues were sensitively dealt with in the reconstruction, where blocks were put in their original place wherever possible.

The rebuilding of the temple itself was carried out according to ancient techniques, with no cement or mortar to set the blocks, and where lubricant was needed to move the blocks into place, Aswan clay was used which self-levelled into any dips and depressions in the masonry.[43] The conservationist's task was simplified by the hundreds of years of floodwater running through the temple, as it removed the painted decoration. Although tragic for the temple, as it was visible at the start of the century, it meant painted murals did not need to be considered with the re-erection project. Kalabsha was reconstructed on a site with the temple of Beit al-Wali, the Kiosk of Qertassi and the Chapel of Dedwen, in a landscaped area designed to be close in appearance to the original site. This was achieved for the most part, with the only environmental difference being that the original site of Kalabsha was on sandstone whereas the new site was granite.

Like Kalabsha, the Aswan Dam had submerged Philae from December to mid-summer, with only the cornice of the pylon visible (fig. 59). Once the water subsided the walls were covered in slime and required cleaning and conservation. By a twist of fate this submersion saved the temples from damage by sandstorms and washed the temple walls clean of salts that have proved so destructive to other temples in Egypt.[44] After Lake Nasser was created, without intervention, Philae would have been permanently submerged. John F. Kennedy and the US Congress donated $6 million, assuring its safety and preservation.[45]

The Philae rescue project was carried out by Egyptian engineers using Swedish, French, German and British consultants and financing. It cost £7.5 million, of which £650,000 came from the British Museum and the revenue of the Exhibition of the Treasures of Tutankhamun.[46] In the early 1970s it was moved to the island of Agilqiyya which was not submerged by Lake Nasser, and was 457m north-west of Philae. The top of the island was blasted in order to give it roughly the same shape as the original location, and was dismantled and rebuilt block by block.

59 Philae temple during the inundation. (*Reproduced with permission of the Griffith Institute, University of Oxford*)

60 Temple of Ramses II at Abu Simbel (after the move)

The monuments that have received the most publicity, however, are the two temples at Abu Simbel, that of Ramses II (fig. 60) and his wife Nefertari (fig. 61). These temples were carved directly from the living cliff face and posed a problem as to the best way of conserving them. Various ideas were suggested, including one by William MacQuitty with an element of fairy tale about it. He suggested producing an Atlantis-like site. He believed the temples could be left *in situ* by enclosing them with a membrane of reinforced concrete that kept clean water next to the temple. Lifts and walkways would be included within the membrane so people could visit and the water could be purified by using a filter.[47] Needless to say, this idea was considered too elaborate to consider. Another idea was to build a high wall around it, damming the water from the lake, or an Italian suggestion involved raising the two rock masses forming the temples as whole blocks and placing them slightly higher. This scheme was considered too expensive and was abandoned in 1962;[48] it was decided it would be cheaper to cut the temple into small pieces and transport them block by block.

This scheme cost in the region of $32 million and donations came from Pope John XXIII ($10,000), the State of Qatar ($40,000), the US Congress ($4 million) and within 12 months a further 23 countries donated $1,712,000 to the project.[49] Egypt showed its gratitude for these donations by stating foreign contributors would be granted excavation rights proportionate to their donation. Britain only donated £28,000 and therefore British archaeology suffered as a result.[50] Abu Simbel was once more opened to the public in September 1968, after it had been completely dismantled and moved to higher ground, reassembled inside two concrete domes covered by an artificial hill.[51]

Despite the rescue of these few large monuments many were lost forever, including temples, tombs and prehistoric rock art and burials which could provide a link between the Nubian and Egyptian cultures and how they developed. There was a five-year campaign for archaeological research to take place before the sluices were opened for the first time. This was nowhere near enough time to strategically record 360km of land on both sides of the Nile. Therefore, a process was developed where some archaeological groups excavated, some took extensive photographs and others concentrated on publishing all known research on the Nubian area to ensure the monuments became public knowledge. This was never going to be enough but it was the best that could be achieved in the time.

Despite the difficulties, the construction of the High Dam was the first time that the course of the Nile had been changed by man, and it is not only a great achievement but has also been beneficial to Egypt as 35,000 square miles of land have been reclaimed for farming.[52] A new Valley Project was formed, which over the next 15 years will further multiply by five the cultivated land of Egypt, although this requires three times the total discharge of the Nile,[53] and would be a huge but effective undertaking. There is also a comprehensive master plan to deal with increasing social problems such as housing, population growth and the clearing of pollution on all beaches and recreational lakes.[54] When Sir Alfred Milner stated 'In Egypt, prosperity and water go hand in hand'[55] he was accurately summarising 100 years of economical and political growth based around the Nile and the manipulation of water.

The innovations of the eighteenth, nineteenth and twentieth centuries have made a huge impact on the economy of Egypt, and at the close of the nineteenth century Egypt's assets were 1223km of railway and an adequate number of engines and rolling stock, 3218km of telegraph lines, six new gun boats, barges and control of the whole of Sudan.[56] Since Mohammed Ali planted the cotton cash crop, this now occupies a fifth of the agricultural land in Egypt. For a while

61 Temple of Nefertari at Abu Simbel (after the move)

it was the only export but has since been followed by rice, maize and sugarcane, with less attention being paid to subsistence crops, resulting in a shortfall of feeding the 63 million people of Egypt (projected to rise to 100 million by 2030).[57] Once more the Nile and the new High Dam are at their capacity, but evidence has demonstrated again and again that with careful management of the Nile these things can be overcome.

WHOEVER DRINKS
WATER FROM THE NILE
IS SURE TO RETURN

From the preceding chapters it is clear the Nile has maintained an important role in the development of the Egyptian culture from the earliest period to the modern day. Although the use of the Nile has changed over the centuries, it was and still is essential for food production in the form of agriculture and fishing, practicalities such as transportation and a water source, and leisure in the form of swimming and boating. This consistency of use in an ever-changing culture says a great deal about the river and how important it is for the developing communities living on her banks. Regardless of the function of the river there is no denying it is a constant feature in the lives of the people of Egypt, ancient and modern, and without it the history of Egypt would be very different.

So after tracing the history of the use of the Egyptian Nile from 5000 BCE to the modern day, what does the future hold for the Nile and Egypt? The answer to this question is held in the past, and in the previous pages of this book; the future of Egypt and the Nile continues to be one of agricultural cash crops and tourism. The difficulty here is ensuring that these do not overlap with one having a detrimental effect on the other. This is something that to date has not reached a happy medium, as all of the places mentioned in this book, from the pyramids to the Islamic mosques and churches, are under threat, either from natural causes, the encroachment of urbanisation or manmade damage. As tourism is so essential to the economy of Egypt it is paramount that these monuments are preserved.

Each site needs to be individually assessed, as they are affected by different threats which need to be identified before individual management plans can be introduced, ensuring the site is protected and conserved for future generations. However, it is important to balance the interests of the economy, natural resources, cultural preservation, aesthetic requirements and social and political restraints.[1]

Sometimes the plans initiated are controversial and seem to benefit tourists over the needs of the native Egyptians, and a prime example is the destruction of the village of El Gourna over the Valley of the Nobles in Luxor. These houses were on the site for over 150 years and some in themselves were considered historical sites, but due to damage which has been caused to the tombs, including theft, water damage and vibrations, this village was earmarked for demolition and the villagers re-housed.

Further work in Luxor started in 2008 in the remodelling of the East Bank Cornice at Luxor, which involved widening the road, creating larger coach parks and providing a walk way down by the river, which seems to be in direct conflict to Hawass' comment in 1998 that 'Luxor is a unique city. Its atmosphere of quiet, ancient streets, and culturally special people should be preserved.'[2] The centre of Luxor is to become a tourist centre, with shopping centres, restaurants and parking facilities, losing the character that people have loved about Luxor for decades. The victims of this construction, in addition to the locals, are the buildings along the cornice, which are to be or have been demolished, including some beautiful nineteenth-century colonial buildings, Chicago House losing half its garden and the Mecure Etap losing its front wing to the demolition ball; all these buildings have a role to play in the history of Luxor and Egypt as a whole. Whilst traffic from tourism is a problem, especially with up to 250 coaches a day on trips from the Red Sea, is turning the scenic cornice into a giant coach park the way to deal with it? Not everyone agrees it is. Many Egyptologists believe this project is designed to segregate tourists from the locals rather than enabling them to interact with Egyptians in their own home environment. Segregation only ever brings misunderstanding, bitterness and confrontation.

The additional tourists expected to visit Luxor means there will be even more traffic and cruise boats to deal with, and already people complain the view of the Nile is marred by cruise boats in dock, as well as oil and pollution being pumped into the river. In the nineteenth century they complained of the Thomas Cook steamers in front of the Winter Palace, but that was 'scenic' in comparison to the three or four deep cruise ships docked on the east bank at any one time today. To solve this problem, the authorities have proposed a new cruise ship port to be constructed further south past the bridge, moving the boats from central Luxor. Whilst making for more scenic photographs from central Luxor, how will the new proposed site affect the farmers and villagers who live near the proposed sites?

Tourists, whilst bringing in revenue, also cause a great deal of damage to the monuments – some deliberate in the form of graffiti or even chipping bits from the monuments to take home as souvenirs. One wonders how many 'bits of pyramid' are currently languishing in tourists' lofts. Other damage is not so intentional, such as bag buckles and spokes from umbrellas scratching the walls of monuments, or even levels of humidity in the tombs of the Valley of the Kings, for example, which rises dramatically throughout the day affecting the paint and plaster work within the tombs which ultimately leads to many tombs being closed. As an avid traveller to the Valley of the Kings, I find it heartbreaking to see thousands of people filing into tombs, marching to the end and marching out, often without even looking at the images their breath and very presence is causing irreparable damage to. The temples of Abu Simbel, for example, often cater for 2000 tourists every 90 minutes, and the vibrations from their feet, voices and the changing humidity levels caused a block to fall from the ceiling from the Ramses temple in recent years. The answer to this ever-growing problem is not easy, with many archaeologists favouring building life-size replicas of the tombs some distance from the Valley and closing the real ones in order to conserve them. Many visitors to the Valley probably would not notice the difference. In 2005 the tomb of Thutmosis III was reconstructed accurately, including the damage and general tomb condition, and went on tour. The reconstruction was almost perfect and was an opportunity to study the tomb without causing damage to it. However, most tourists are not looking at the monuments themselves, but just wish to tick them from the 'must-see' lists.

Some monuments are not being damaged purely by tourism, but also by the environment, and there are a number that were for centuries above the water level for the majority of the year, but are now in danger from sewage and runoff from agricultural fields, creating a high water table and resulting in the monuments being saturated with water.[3] At Karnak and Luxor temples, the monuments are being damaged by not only a high water table but also salt-laden ground water running from the sugar cane fields (fig. 62). Urban and agricultural development exacerbates the problem[4] and from month to month carved reliefs are crumbling or becoming unreadable (fig. 63). After the flash floods in the autumn of 1994, lower parts of the walls at Karnak were so encrusted with salt that the decoration was obliterated and images which could be read then, cannot be read today.[5] The problems are not improving and in 2001 new cracks developed in the pylon at Luxor temple which have to be monitored carefully for movement and changes.[6] From 1999 a Swedish study (SWECO) has been concentrating on identifying a long-term solution for the problem, necessitating a good water-management system, using less water for irrigation and using lined canals for drainage.[7] In the short term it was considered essential to lower the ground water and in 2006 USAID (United States Agency for International Development) funded a project to do this at both Karnak and Luxor. These sites are also carefully monitored with the remaining reliefs being observed, rapidly recorded and cleaned.

The same problems affecting Luxor and Karnak in the south are prevalent in the north as well, and at Giza pools of water were forming in the Valley Temple of Khafre, where studies showed the water level had risen to over 15m above sea level. Since 2008 a series of pumps have been installed at the site pumping about 7000 cubic metres of water a day, and the water level has since dropped almost a metre.[8] Conservation work has been carried out on the Sphinx, as it is unstable and over the last decade blocks have fallen to the ground. The Sphinx in recent years has been given new paws, where new blocks have been built around the original paws (fig. 64).

Other problems affecting the monuments of Egypt can be found at the harbour of Alexandria which has a great deal to offer archaeologists, divers and tourists in general, although it is not well visited by Westerners at present. The ever-rising sea levels are changing the coastline of Egypt and should the sea level continue to rise, as global warming has threatened, only a 1.5m increase would submerge modern Alexandria.[9] This was a problem that affected those in the past and beneath the waves, in addition to the Pharos Lighthouse and the Ptolemaic royal quarters, are at least three French wrecks from the 1798 Battle of the Nile, *L'Orient*, *Le Guerrier* and the frigate *L'Artémise*, and it is said that on still days their masts are visible in the water.[10] These coastal sites are not popular tourist attractions because of the inaccessibility of the remains, and many divers complain of

Above left: 62 Water damage to north wall of hypostyle hall, Karnak

Above right: 63 Damage caused by salt, Karnak

the poor visibility here; partially because of the rough waters but also because of sewage pumped directly into the sea.

This sewage problem was addressed amongst other issues at the International Workshop on Submarine Archaeology and Coastal Management (SARCOM) in April 1997, attended by an interdisciplinary team, UNESCO and the Ministry of Culture.[11] At the time of the conference, over a third of all Alexandria's waste water and untreated sewage was pumped directly into the eastern harbour, with the other two-thirds being dumped into Lake Mariot to the south. Both the lake and the harbour are both heavily polluted, and Dr Nariman Mostafa Soheil from the Alexandria General Organisation for Sanitary Drainage stated the outfalls at Qaitbey and El Silsila were to be closed in 2003, although a secondary treatment plant will not be complete until 2010.[12] The archaeological sites cannot be made available to the public until this sewage problem is addressed and early completion of this is encouraged. Beyali Hosni El-Beyali, a consultant for the Water and Drainage Department, has since announced that three main sewerage outlets into the archaeological area of the eastern harbour were closed and were only to be opened to drain rainwater after heavy storms.[13] On the strength of these initial closures, four diving companies were opened in October 2001, allowing diving over the Pharos area, although they are not allowed further into the harbour because the pollution is still very bad. However in 2006, the visibility at the Pharos site remained poor due to the pollution, making it almost impossible to see the structures beneath the waves.

Other problems with the remains under the eastern harbour were caused in 1993 when, in an attempt to preserve the Qaitbey Citadel, 180 concrete blocks weighing 7–20 tons each were dumped into the sea 30m from the Citadel, creating a breakwater. Adequate research had not been done prior to this and it was discovered afterwards they had been dropped directly over the remains of the Pharos Lighthouse. In order to try and preserve some of these remains before 1997, over 2000 artefacts and architectural elements were excavated from the seabed in this region; some were put on display at Kom el Dikka (fig. 65) and others went to Berlin. These finds and the destruction caused by the concrete blocks led to the organisation of the SARCOM Workshop in April 1997. The workshop, amongst other things, addressed the problems of the concrete blocks over the Pharos and a programme was devised for their removal. Ten were raised in 1996, 45 in February 1998 and remaining blocks in January 2001. The site was now ready for archaeological exploration.[14] This was to prove to be quite a feat as much of the royal palace was under fill used in mid nineteenth century to compensate for subsidence,[15] and some of the eastern harbour is covered by modern piers, breakwaters and Cape Silsila.[16]

The possibilities of how to make the underwater structures accessible to tourists was also discussed at the workshop and three suggestions were presented,

Above left: 64 The Sphinx's new feet. Giza

Above right: 65 Underwater finds from Alexandria at Kom el Dikka, Alexandria

starting with the idea of draining the harbour and exposing the remains. This naturally was rejected. At the death of Adul-Sadat in 1984 and Dumas in 1985, it had been decided to build a museum in Abu Qir for the objects and two labs for the treatment of metal and non-metal objects brought up from the seabed.[17] This idea was embellished and Ali Radwan, the Head of the General Union of Arab Archaeologists, suggested a museum built on two levels: one on the shore displaying the artefacts already rescued from the seabed, and the other as a floating museum using either a U-boat or a glass-bottomed boat to view the underwater items.[18] These proposals were also rejected because their movement through and under the water could threaten the archaeology, changing the topography of the sites.[19] The idea of the museum has been embraced and Abdel Moneim claimed it would be 'one of the world's modern wonders'. The finer details are still being discussed and three rather than two floors are being considered; one floor is to be an onshore building with artefacts from Alexandria as a whole, the second floor to show artefacts from the seabed exhibited in aquariums, and the third an underwater tunnel going through the Ptolemaic city.[20] However, the plexiglass tunnel has been criticised as it would limit the visitor to only one archaeological zone,[21] whereas there are numerous sites in the area. The start-up costs, the level of technology and the finance required for the annual maintenance are immense and would need to be considered.

At present there are 2.2 million tourists[22] from Egypt and the Middle East to Alexandria annually; the authorities want to develop the eastern harbour to attract Western tourists creating further revenue: 'Once the underwater archaeological museum has been developed and the area has been cleared of polluting sediments and the city's wastewater is properly treated, Alexandria will become a centre of cultural tourism.'[23]

This future construction relies on a lot of uncertainties and it will be interesting to see how this project develops. In the meantime, work continues on the archaeology of the sites in order to survey the eastern harbour, especially the Ptolemaic city. 'Sub-scan Sonar' is being developed at Woods Hole Oceanographic Institute, supported by the US navy, which will help to produce a 3D image of the area,[24] as well as extracting cores useful for dating purposes[25] and tracing environmental change. A desk-top study is being carried out to try to recreate the monuments, especially the lighthouse, using the finds, contemporary images, mosaics and texts to create an accurate reproduction,[26] all of which will add to the presentation of the artefacts in the new museums. This museum will bring more tourists to Alexandria and Egypt in general, which will help the Egyptian economy.

The water from the Nile itself is also causing irreparable damage to the monuments, which has been the focus of many archaeological expeditions, as conservation is the only way of preserving the monuments for future generations. This may be essential to the continuation of tourism to Egypt, as well as the survival of the people who live in the Nile Valley. If the Nile no longer existed, should it dry out or continue to drift to the east, then tourism and therefore the economy of Egypt will dwindle and disappear altogether. So even though most tourists see the Nile as little more than a pretty backdrop for their photographs, without it the majority of the sites would become inaccessible and the hoards of coaches and visitors would disappear as few would be dedicated enough to overcome the difficulties of desert-based monuments. The drying up of the Nile is not as far-fetched as one may think; over the centuries various canals have dried up resulting in a vastly reduced water flow than in antiquity, although there are more distributaries in the Delta region now than there were in the time of Herodotus and Strabo.[27] Over the centuries, the capital of Egypt has moved, especially in the Memphite area, due to the migration of the Nile, shifting from Memphis, Babylon, el Fustat, Cairo and Heliopolis. As the Nile in each area was suddenly left dry, it was impossible to survive,[28] indicating that the Nile dictated where the major cities could be supported. As the Nile is moving at a rate of approximately 9km every 1000 years, with regional fluctuations such as movement of only 2km at Luxor,[29] without artificial irrigation the capital city and major sites may be forced to move. In the same manner as the Nile is still migrating, Egypt still suffers from flash floods which can destroy a harvest and have occurred frequently over the last 200 years – 1799, 1818, 1820s 1883, 1898, 1905, 1910, 1914,

1915, October 1916, October 1917, October 1918, 1979, October 1994, October 2001, 21 January 2008 and February 2010. These floods are unpredictable because they are so localised,[30] so although the Egyptians have checked the floods with the High Dam they are still at the mercy of the environment, and are in that way the same as the ancient Egyptians, with water being the pivot of their survival. The Nile is utilised today in the same way it has been for thousands of years, and although in the last 200 years the Nile is no longer used as the main highway with the introduction of the train and air travel, it is still sometimes considered the cheapest and easiest way of moving goods and people.[31] It seems the Egyptians today are as reliant on the Nile as they were 7000 years ago and it is likely they will continue to be so for 7000 years to come. However, despite its very utilitarian function, the Nile has retained its romantic image in the saying that 'Whoever drinks from the Nile is sure to return'. Although most travel guides strongly advise against drinking the Nile water, it is the only water source in the area, so anyone who has an ice cube or food washed and cooked in tap water is indeed drinking of the Nile, and it is true to say the more Egyptian tap water you drink, the more your body becomes immune to it and you are more inclined to return to the land of the pharaohs.

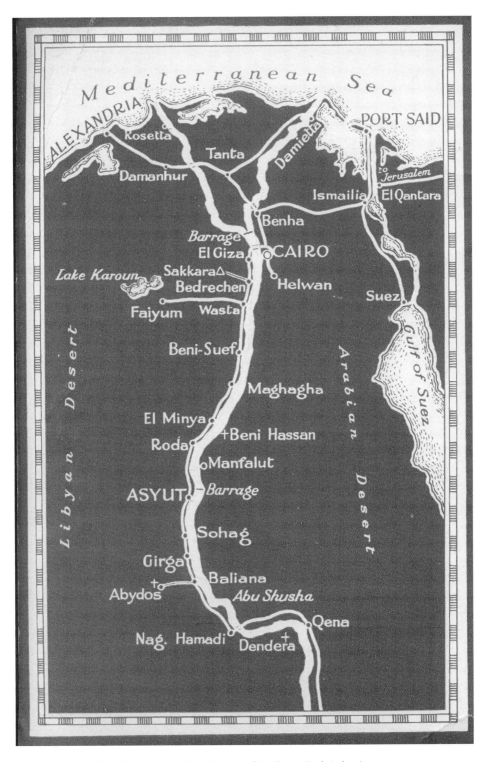

Opposite: MAP 1 The Nile valley in 1863. (*Courtesy of the Thomas Cook Archives*)

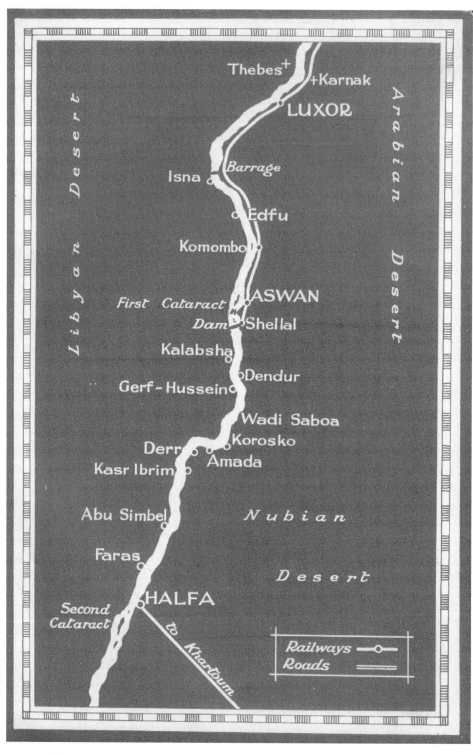

MAP 2 Upper Egypt in 1864. (*Courtesy of the Thomas Cook Archives*)

NOTES

INTRODUCTION

1   Quoted by E. Wilson in *The Century Magazine*, 1887.

1 WE NEED NOT SLEEP TO DREAM

1   Manley, D. (1991) *The Nile: A Traveller's Anthology*, London, Cassell, p.14.
2   Jules Verne.
3   Kerisel, J. (1999) *The Nile and its Masters; past, present and future*, Rotterdam, A.A. Balkema, p.31.
4   Booth, C. (2009) *The Mummy's Curse and other Mysteries*, Oxford, Oneworld Publications, pp.142–58.
5   Meinardus, O. (1962) *The Holy Family in Egypt*, from http://www.coptic.net/articles/HolyFamilyInEgypt.txt.
6   Hart, G. (1986) *A Dictionary of Gods and Goddesses*, London, Routledge, p.75.
7   Lurker, M. (1974) *The Gods and Symbols of Ancient Egypt*, London, Thames and Hudson, p.57.
8   Lichtheim, M. (1975) *Ancient Egyptian Literature*, Vol. 1, Berkeley, University of California Press, pp.204–9.
9   Little, (1965), p.18.
10 Tafla, B. (2000) 'The Father of Rivers: The Nile in Ethiopian Literature' in Erlich, H. and Gershoni, I. (eds) *The Nile; histories, cultures, myths*, London, Lynne Reinner Publishers, p.166.
11 Arbel, B. (2000) 'Renaissance Geographical Literature and the Nile' in Erlich, H. and Gershoni, I. (eds) *The Nile; histories, cultures, myths*, London, Lynne Reinner Publishers, p.106.
12 Arbel (2000), p.107.
13 Collins (2001), p.15.
14 Faulkner, R.O. (1998) *The Ancient Egyptian Pyramid Texts*, Oxford, Clarendon Press, p.235.
15 Collins (2001), p.18.
16 Arbel (2000), p.106.
17 Tafla (2000), p.162.
18 Collins (2001), p.164.
19 Lichtheim (1975), p.186–9.

2 AN ANCIENT RIVER STILL EVOLVING IN MANY WAYS

1   Collins (2001), p.1.
2   Ibid., p.14.

3   Trigger, B. (1983) 'The Rise of the Egyptian Civilisation' in Trigger, B. et al (eds) *Ancient Egypt; a social history*, Cambridge, Cambridge University Press, p.9.

4   Petrie, W.M.F. and Quibell, J.E. (1895) *Naqada and Ballas*, London, B. Quaritch.

5   Petrie, W.M.F. (1896) *Naqada and Ballas*, London. B. Quaritch.

6   Spencer, A.J. (1993) *Early Egypt; the rise of civilisation in the Nile Valley*, London, British Museum Press, p.9.

7   Trigger (1983), p.2.

8   Spencer (1993), p.9.

9   Trigger (1983), p.3.

10 Ibid., p.16.

11 Wengrow, D. (2006) *The Archaeology of Early Egypt*, Cambridge, Cambridge University Press, p.84.

12 Trigger (1983), pp.17, 19.

13 Ibid., p.29.

14 Midant-Reynes (2002), p.110.

15 Wengrow (2006), p.80.

16 Spencer (1993), p.20.

17 Trigger (1983), p.22.

18 Spencer (1993), p.20.

19 Van Neer, W. (1986) 'Some notes on the fish remains from Wadi Kubbaniya (Upper Egypt: Late Paeleolithic)' in Brinkhuizen, D.C. and Clason, A.T. (eds) *Fish and Archaeology: Studies in Osteometry, Taphonomy, Seasonality and Fishing Methods*, Oxford, p.104.

20 Midant-Reynes, B. (2000) *The Prehistory of Egypt from the First Egyptians to the First Pharaohs*, Oxford, Blackwell Publishers, p.106.

21 Trigger, (1983), p.18.

22 Ibid., p.26.

23 Baines and Malek (1980), p.30.

24 Wengrow (2006), pp.27, 48.

25 Ibid., p.29.

26 Ibid., p.51.

27 Spencer (1993), p.25.

28 Wengrow (2006), p.51.

29 Trigger (1983), p.29.

30 Wengrow (2006), p.54.

31 Spencer (1993), p.25.

32 Wengrow (2006), pp.27, 51.

33 Petrie, W.M.F. (1901) *Diospolis Parva*, London, Bernard Quaritch, p.21.

34 Spencer (1993), p.24.

35 Baines and Malek (1980), p.30.

36 Midant-Reynes (2002), p.235.

37 Wengrow (2006), p.99.

38 Wilkinson, T.A.H. (1999) *Early Dynastic Egypt*, London, Routledge, p.30.

39 Wengrow (2006), p.75.

40 Wilkisnon (1999), p.35.

41 Partridge, R. (1996) *Transport in Ancient Egypt*, London, Rubicon Press, p.17.

42 Wengrow (2006), p.115.

43 Ibid., p.116.

44 Ibid., p.118.

45 Jones, J. (2002) *Towards mummification; new evidence for early developments in Egyptian Archaeology* 21, p.6.

46 Wengrow (2006), p.121.

47 Ibid., p.123.

3 CIVILISATION WITHOUT CITIES

1   Rice, M. (1989) *Egypt's Making; The Origins of Ancient Egypt*, London, Routledge, p.39.
2   Ibid., p.39.
3   Krzyżaniak, L. (1977) *Early farming cultures on the lower Nile: the pre-dynastic period in Egypt*, Editions scientifiques de Pologne, p.128.
4   Aldred, C. (1965) *Egypt to the end of the Old Kingdom*, London, Thames & Hudson, p.40.
5   Midant-Reynes (2002), p.237.
6   Wengrow (2006), p.87.
7   Wilkinson (2002), p.516.
8   Rice (1989), p.34.
9   Wilkinson (1999), p.40.
10 Bard, K. (2000) 'The Emergence of the Egyptian State' in Shaw, I. (ed.) *The Oxford History of Ancient Egypt*, Oxford, Oxford University Press, p.64.
11 Hartung, U. (2002) 'Imported Jars from Cemetary U at Abydos and the relations between Egypt and Canaan in Predynastic times' in Van den Brink, E. and Levy, T. (eds) *Egypt and the Levant : interrelations from the 4th through the early 3rd millennium BCE*, London, Leicester University Press, p.437.
12 Ibid., p.443.
13 Bard (2000), p.73.
14 Rice (1989), p.37.
15 Krzyżaniak (1977), p.130.
16 Aldred (1965), p.36.
17 Partridge (1996), p.24.
18 Ibid., p.55.
19 O'Connor, D. (1995) 'The Earliest Royal Boat Graves' in *Egyptian Archaeology* 6, p.5.
20 Bard (2000), p.74.
21 Malek, J. (2000) 'The Old Kingdom' in Shaw, I. (ed.) *The Oxford History of Ancient Egypt*, Oxford, Oxford University Press, p.95.
22 Midant-Reynes (2002), p.244.
23 Ibid., p.246.
24 Bard (2000), p.65.
25 Midant-Reynes (2002), p.246.
26 Currently in the Ashmolean Museum, Oxford. Fragments of two other mace-heads of the same period can be found in the Petrie Museum.
27 Book 2, p.99.
28 Midant-Reynes (2002), p.248.
29 Bard (2000), p.68 .
30 Ibid., p.69.
31 Krzyżaniak (1977), p.132.
32 Ibid., p.140.
33 Rice (1989), p.50.
34 A *serekh* was a rectangular box representative of the palace with the king's name written within.
35 Midant-Reynes (2002), p.232.
36 Rice (1989), p.51.
37 Clayton, P. (1994) *Chronicle of the Pharoahs*, London, Thames & Hudson, p.29.
38 Rice (1989), p.50.
39 Brewer, D. and Friedman, R. (1989) *Fish and Fishing in Ancient Egypt*, Warminster, Aris and Phillips, p.2.
40 Rice (1989), p.49.
41 Ibid., p.51.

42 Stevenson-Smith, W. (1994) *The art and architecture of ancient Egypt*, London, Yale University Press, p.10.

43 Bard (2000), p.82.

44 Rice (1989), p.54.

45 Midant-Reynes (2002), p.248.

46 Bard (2000), p.70.

47 Ibid., p.72.

48 Ibid., p.71.

49 Ibid., p.72.

50 Wilkinson (1999), p.37.

51 Krzyżaniak (1977), p.135.

52 Ibid., p.129.

53 Midant-Reynes (2002), p.237.

54 Ibid., p.247.

55 Postgate, N., Wang, T. and Wilkinson, T. (1995) 'The evidence for early writing: utilitarian or ceremonial' in *Antiquity* 69, p.458.

56 Krzyżaniak (1977), p.147.

57 Postgate et al (1995), p.465.

58 Bard (2000), p.78.

59 Ibid., p.81.

60 Aldred (1965), p.63.

61 Bard (2000), p.78.

62 Rice (1989), p.63.

4 THE DESERT IS DYING OF HUNGER

1 Eyre, C. (1999) 'The Village Economy in Pharaonic Egypt' in Bowman, A. and Rogan, E. (1999) *Agriculture in Egypt: from pharaonic to modern times*, Oxford, Oxford University Press, p.33.

2 Ibid., p.35.

3 Hassan, F. (1993) 'Town and Village in ancient Egypt: Ecology, society and urbanization' in Shaw, T., Sinclair P., Andah B. and Okpoko A. (eds) *The Archaeology of Africa; food metals and towns*, London, Routledge, p.560.

4 Ibid., p.554.

5 Eyre (1999), p.40.

6 Aldred (1965), pp.54–5.

7 *The Histories* translated by Sélincourt, A. (1954) *Herodotus; the Histories*, London, Penguin, p.139, Herodotus Book 2, p.99.

8 Jeffreys, D. (2009) *Memphis and beyond; climate change in ancient Egypt*, EES Seminar, 17 October 2009.

9 Kerisel (1999), p.45.

10 Hassan (1993), p.555.

11 Wodzińska, A. (2007) 'Main Street Ceramics' in Lehner, M. and Wetterstrom, W. (eds) *Giza Reports: the Giza Plateau Mapping Project*, Vol. 1, Research Associates Inc., Boston, p.143.

12 Abd el-Aziz, A. (2007) 'Gallery III.4 Excavations' in Lehner, M. and Wetterstrom, W. (eds) *Giza Reports: the Giza Plateau Mapping Project*, Vol. 1, Ancient Egypt, Research Associates Inc., Boston, p.196.

13 Lehner, M. (2007) 'Introduction to gallery III.4 Excavations' in Lehner, M. and Wetterstrom, W. (eds) *Giza Reports: the Giza Plateau Mapping Project*, Vol. 1, Ancient Egypt, Research Associates Inc., Boston, pp.190–2.

14 Hawass, Z. (2006) *Mountains of the Pharoahs*, Cairo, Cairo University Press, p.164.

15 Hawass (2006), p.166; Lehner, M. (1992) 'Excavations at Giza 1988-1991; the location and importance of the pyramid settlement' in *Oriental Institute News and Notes*, No 135 (fall) 1992, accessed at http://oi.uchicago.edu/research/pubs/nn/fal92_giz.html.

16 Jackson, K. and Stamp, J. (2002) *Pyramid; Beyond Imagination*, London BBC Worldwide Ltd, p.34.

17 Ibid., p.78.

18 Jackson & Stamp (2002), p.33; Mendelssohn, K. (1974) *The Riddle of the Pyramids*, London. Sphere Books Ltd, p.130; Edwards, I.E.S. (1947/1993) *The pyramids of Egypt*, London, Penguin Books, p.277.

19 Herodotus Book 2, p.99.

20 Jeffreys, D. (2001) 'High and Dry? Survey of the Memphite escarpment' in *Egyptian Archaeology* 19, p.16.

21 Lutley, K. and Bunbury, J. (2008) 'The Nile on the Move' in *Egyptian Archaeology* 32 (spring), p.5.

22 Bunbury, J. (2009) *Memphis and beyond; climate change in ancient Egypt*, EES Seminar, 17 October 2009.

23 Malek (2000), p.96.

24 Ibid., p.108.

25 Faulkner, R.O. (1969) *The Ancient Egyptian Pyramid Texts*, Oxford, Clarendon Press, p.154.

26 Utterance 473 describes the king crossing the celestial river.

27 Rossi, C. (2004) *Mathematics and Architecture in Ancient Egypt*, Cambridge, Cambridge University Press, p.182.

28 Ibid., p.184.

29 Eyre (1999), p.49.

30 Malek (2000), p.102.

31 Eyre (1999), p.52.

32 Fairbridge, R. (1963) 'Nile Sedimentation above Wadi Halfa during the last 20,000 years' in *KUSH* 11 33, p.102.

34 Malek (2000), p.107.

35 Kerisel (1999), p.52.

36 Partridge (1996), p.3.

37 Kerisel (1999), p.55.

38 Hassan (1993), p.567.

39 Ibid., p.565.

40 Decker (1987) *Sport and Games of Ancient Egypt*, London, Yale University Press, p.102.

41 Brewer and Friedman (1989), p.24.

42 Ibid., p.15.

43 Partridge (1996), p.22.

44 Collins (2001), p.18.

45 Bunbury (2009).

46 Hassan (2007), p.367.

47 Admonitions of Ipuwer, lines 3, 6, 9–10.

48 Collins (2001), p.18.

5 THE FLOOD AS LAND TO MY FEET

1 Hillier, J.K., Bunbry, J.M. and Graham, A. (2007) 'Monuments on a Migrating Nile' in *Journal of Archaeological Science* 34, p.1012.

2 Ibid., p.1013.

3 Graham, A. and Bunbury, J. (2005) 'The ancient landscapes and waterscapes of Karnak' in *Egyptian Archaeology* 27 (Autumn), p.17.

4 Graham and Bunbury (2005), p.18.

5 Hillier et al (2007), p.1014.

6 Bunbury et al (2008), p.351.

7   Ibid., p.356.
8   Eyre, C. (1994) 'The water regime for Orchards and Plantations in Pharaonic Egypt' in *Journal of Egyptian Archaeology* 80, p.75.
9   Bunbury et al (2008), p.369.
10 Bunbury (2009).
11 Graffiti from the Valley of the Queens.
12 Vinson, S. (1996) *The Nile Boatmen at Work 1200 BCE–400 CE*, Baltimore, Maryland, UMI Dissertation Services, p.87.
13 Cross, S.W. (2009) 'The Hydrology of the Valley of the Kings, Egypt' in *The Heritage of Egypt*, Vol. 2, No 1, Issue 4, p.7.
14 Ibid., p.8.
15 Ibid., p.9.
16 Ray, J. (2007) *The Rosetta Stone; and the rebirth of Ancient Egypt*, London, Profile, p.9.
17 Reeves, N. and Wilkinson, R. (1996) *The Complete Valley of the Kings*, London, Thames and Hudson, p.25.
18 Eyre (1994), p.75.
19 Baines and Malek (1980), p.17.
20 Kozloff, A.P., Bryan, B.M. and Berman, L.M. (1992) *Egypt's Dazzling Sun: Amenhotep III and his world* 21, Cleveland, Cleveland Museum of Art in co-operation with Indiana University Press, p.72.
21 Kemp (1994), p.216.
22 Decker (1987), p.148.
23 Lichtcheim (1975), p.189.
24 David, R. and Tapp, E. (1984) *Evidence embalmed: modern medicine and the mummies of ancient Egypt*, Manchester, Manchester University Press, p.95.
25 Booth, C. (2006) 'A study of a Ptolemaic head in the Petrie Museum' in *Journal of Egyptian Archaeology* 91.
26 Brewer and Friedman (1989), p.9.
27 Lichtheim, M. (1976) *Ancient Egyptian Literature*, Berkeley, University of California Press, p.193.
28 Eyre (1994), p.64.
29 Arnold, D. (2003) *The encyclopaedia of ancient Egyptian architecture*, London, Tauris, p.206.
30 Strudwick, N. and Strudwick, H. (1999) *Thebes in Egypt*, London, British Museum Press, p.46.
31 Wilkinson (2000), p.72.
32 Weeks, K. (2005) *The Illustrated Guide to Luxor; tombs, temples, and museums*, Cairo, The American University in Cairo Press, p.101.
33 Budge, E.A.W (1901) *The Nile; Notes for Travellers in Egypt*, London, Thomas Cook and Sons Ltd, p.91.
34 Partridge (1996), p.63.
35 Ibid., p.7.
36 Ray, J. (2001) *Reflections of Osiris; Lives from Ancient Egypt*, London, Profile, p.55.
37 Tyldesley, J. (1996) *Hatchepsit; the female Pharoah*, London, Penguin Books, p.161.
38 Ibid., p.145.
39 Ray (2001), p.50.
40 Clayton (1994), p.107.
41 Tyldesley (1996), p.147.
42 Partridge (1996), p.47.
43 Ibid., pp.61–2.
44 Ibid., p.7.
45 Von Pilgrim, C. (1997) 'The town site of the Island of Elephantine' in *Egyptian Archaeology* 10, p.16.

46 Jeffreys, D. and Smith, H.S. (1988) 'Memphis and the Nile in the New Kingdom: A preliminary attempt at a historical perspective' in Zivie, A.D. (ed.) *Memphis et ses nŽcropoles au Nouvel Empire*, Paris, p.62.

47 Bietak (2009), p.17.

48 Jeffreys (2006), p.37.

49 Bietak, M. (2009) 'Perrunefer: the principal New Kingdom Naval Base' in *Egyptian Archaeology*, p.15.

50 Bietak M. (1979) *Avaris and Pi-Ramesse: Archaeological exploration in the Eastern Nile Delta*, London, Proceedings of the British Academy, p.283.

51 Van Seters, J. (1966) *The Hyksos; A New Investigation*, London, Yale University Press, p.139.

52 Uphill, E.P. (1984) *The Temples of Per Ramesses*, Wiltshire, Aris and Phillips Ltd, p.3.

53 Van Seters (1966), p.137.

54 Habachi, L. (2001) *Tell el Dab'a I. Vienna*, Verlag der Osterreichishen Akademie der Wissenchaften, p.37.

55 Dorner, J. (2000) 'A late Hyksos water-supply system at Ezbet Hilme' in *Egyptian Archaeology* 16 (spring), pp.12–3.

56 Uphill (1984), p.218.

57 Habachi (2001), p.108.

58 Uphill (1984), p.226.

59 Bietak (1979), p.278.

6 GIFT OF THE NILE

1 Taylor, J. (2000) 'The Third Intermediate Period (1069–664 BC)' in Shaw, I. (ed.), *Oxford History of Ancient Egypt*, Oxford, Oxford University Press, p.330.

2 Ibid., p.331.

3 Trigger et al (1983), p.325.

4 Möller, A. (2000) *Naukratis; Trade in Archaic Greece*, Oxford, Oxford University Press, p.27.

5 Tyldesley, J. (2009) *The Pharoahs*, London, Quercus Publishing Ltd, p.176.

6 Taylor (2000), p.339.

7 Ibid., p.233.

8 Tyldesley (2009), p.177.

9 Taylor (2000), p.367.

10 Trigger et al (1983), p.328.

11 Ibid., p.328.

12 Taylor (2000), p.335.

13 Tyldesley (2009), p.180.

14 Taylor (2000), p.351.

15 Ibid., pp.338, 355.

16 Brewer and Friedman (1989), p.17.

17 Ibid., p.4.

18 Tyldesley (2009), p.182.

19 Ibid., p.184.

20 Ibid., p.185.

21 Ibid., p.185.

22 Taylor (2000), p.359.

23 Tyldesley (2009), p.186.

24 Lloyd, A. (2000) 'The Late Period (664–332 BC)' in Shaw, I. (ed.) *The Oxford history of Ancient Egypt*, Oxford, Oxford University Press, p.372.

25 Möller (2000), p.33.

26 Lloyd (2000), p.373.

27 Lloyd (2000), p.381.

28   Herodotus *Histories* II, p.158.

29   Hinz, W. (1975) *Darius und der Suezkanal in Archäologische Mitteilungen aus Iran* 8, p.118.

30   Ibid., p.117.

31   Redmount, C.A. (1995) 'The Wadi Tumilat and the "Canal of the Pharoahs"' in *JNEA* 54, No 2, p.129.

32   Ibid., p.130.

33   Hinz (1975), p.117.

34   Redmount (1995), p.134.

35   Lloyd, A.B. (1977) 'Necho and the Red Sea: Some Considerations' in *Journal of Egyptian Archaeology* 63, p.145.

36   Möller (2000), p.32.

37   Clayton (1994), p.196.

38   Trigger et al (1983), p.285.

39   Lloyd (1977), p.149.

40   Ibid., p.153.

41   Lloyd (2000), p.374.

42   Möller (2000), p.183.

43   Ibid., p.199.

44   Trigger et al (1983), p.329.

45   Möller (2000), p.185.

46   Tyldesley (2009), p.191.

47   Lloyd (2000), p.274.

48   Möller (2000), p.212.

49   Trigger et al (1983), p.327.

50   Möller (2000), p.210.

51   Taylor (2000), p.347.

52   Tyldesley (2009), p.191.

53   Clayton (1994), p.197.

54   Lloyd (2000), p.389.

7 A RIVER WITHOUT A SOUL

1   Kerisel (1999), p.84.

2   Thompson (1999), p.107.

3   Lloyd, A. (2000a) 'The Ptolemaic Period (332–30 BC)' in Shaw, I. (ed.) *The Oxford History of Ancient Egypt*, Oxford, Oxford University Press, p.395.

4   Marcos, S.A. (2000) 'Early discoveries of submarine archaeological sites in Alexandria' in Mendelssohn, K. (1974) *The Riddle of the Pyramids*, London, Sphere Books Ltd, p.40.

5   E.M. Foster.

6   El Daly, O. (2005) *Egyptology; the Missing Millennium*, London, University College London, p.32.

7   Ray (2001), p.35.

8   Lloyd (2000a), p.405.

9   Thompson, J. (2009) *A History of Egypt; from the earliest times to the present*, London, p.128.

10   Empereur, J.Y. (2000) 'Underwater Archaeological Investigations of the Ancient Pharos' in Erlich, H. and Gershoni, I. (2000) *The Nile: histories, cultures, myths*, London, Lynne Rienner Publishers, p.57.

11   El Daly (2005), pp.53–4.

12   Ibid., p.117.

13   Empereur, J.Y. (1996a) 'Raising Statues and Blocks from the sea at Alexandria' in *Egyptian Archaeology* 9, p.19.

14   Tyldesley, J. (2009a) *Cleopatra*, London, Profile Books, p.80.

15   Goddio, F. (2000) 'Underwater Archaeological Survey of Alexandria's Eastern Harbour' in

Mostafa, M.H., Grimal, N. and Nakashima, D. (eds) (2000) *Underwater Archaeology and Coastal Management; Focus on Alexandria*, Paris, Unesco Publishing, p.63.

16   Empereur (2000), p.59.

17   Marcos (2000), p.37.

18   Ibid., p.38.

19   Ibid., p.39.

20   Arthur Evans and Weill in Marcos (2000), 39 Bull d'Inst Fran d'Arch Orlanle BIFAI 16:37 1919

21   Khalil E. (2008) 'The Lake Mareotis Research Project' in *Egyptian Archaeology* 33, p.9.

22   Empereur (2000), p.54.

23   Ibid., p.56.

24   Ibid., p.55.

25   Ashton, S.A. (2005) 'In search of Cleopatra's temple' in *Egyptian Archaeology* 27 (Autumn), p.30–1.

26   Wilkinson (2000), p.213.

27   Marcos (2000), p.33.

28   Ibid., p.34.

29   Ibid., p.3.

30   Ibid., p.340.

31   Chauveau, M. (2002) *Cleopatra; beyond the myth*, London, Cornell University Press, p.28.

32   Ibid., p.33.

33   Tyldesley (2009), pp.99–100.

34   Tyldesley (2009a), p.203.

35   Jones, P. (2006) *Cleopatra; a sourcebook*, Norman, University of Oklahoma Press, p.104.

36   Ibid., p.105.

37   Thompson (1999), p.108.

38   Ibid., p.109.

39   Lloyd (2000), p.411.

40   Bingen, J. (2007) *Hellenistic Egypt : monarchy, society, economy, culture*, Edinburgh, Edinburgh University Press, p.149.

41   Juliet du Bouley quoted in Thompson (1999), p.137.

42   Thompson (1999), p.128.

43   Thompson, D. (1999a) 'New and Old in the Ptolmaic Fayyum' in Bowman A. and Rogan E. (1999) *Agriculture in Egypt: from Pharaonic to modern times*, Oxford, Oxford University Press, p.126.

44   Ibid., p.134.

45   Dated to year 27 of Ptolemy II 259 BCE, and is the oldest text of this length from this period.

46   Bingen (2007), p.169.

47   Thompson (1999a), p.130.

48   Ibid., p.135.

49   Ricketts, L. (1992) 'The Administration of the Late Ptolemaic Period' in Johnson, J. (ed.) *Live in a Multi-cultural society: Egypt from Cambyses to Constantine and Beyond*, Chicago, The Oriental Institute of the University of Chicago, p.276.

50   Vinsen (1996), p.207.

51   Ibid., p.206.

52   Ibid., p.211.

53   Lloyd (2000), p.403.

54   Clayton (1994), p.209.

55   Tyldesley (2009), p.200.

56   Ray (2001), p.32.

57   Lloyd (2000), p.399.

58   Seeger, J. and Sidebotham, S. (2005) 'Masa Nakari: an ancient port on the Red Sea' in *Egyptian Archaeology* 26, p.19.

59   Seeger and Sidebotham (2005), p.20.

60 Thompson (1999), p.110.
61 Ibid., p.114.
62 Tyldesley (2009a), p.203.
63 Thompson (1999a), p.132.
64 Clayton (1994), p.211.
65 Lloyd (2000), p.419.
66 Bingen (2007), p.143.

8 THE CROSSROADS OF THE WHOLE WORLD

1   Thompson (2009), p.124.
2   Ibid., pp.137–8.
3   Kerisel (1999), p.7.
4   Tyldesley (2009), p.200.
5   Gabra, G. (1993) *Cairo the Coptic Museum and Old Churches*, Cairo, Egyptian International Publishing Co., p.15.
6   Peacock, D. (2000) 'The Roman Period (30 BC–AD 311)' in Shaw, I. (ed.) *The Oxford History of Ancient Egypt*, Oxford, Oxford University Press, p.423.
7   Ibid., p.445.
8   Rowlandson, J. (1999) 'Agricultural Tenancy and Village Society in Roman Egypt' in Bowman, A. and Rogan, E. (1999) *Agriculture in Egypt: from pharaonic to modern times*, Oxford, Oxford University Press, p.151.
9   Rowlandson (2001), p.142.
10 Ibid., p.145.
11 Banaji, J. (1999) 'Agrarian History and the Labour Organisation of Byzantine Large Estate' in Bowman, A. and Rogan, E. (1999) *Agriculture in Egypt: from pharaonic to modern times*, Oxford, Oxford University Press, p.200.
12 Banaji (2001), p.201.
13 Peacock (2000), p.424.
14 Eyre (1994), pp.60–1.
15 Thompson (1999a), p.133.
16 Thompson (1999), p.123.
17 Peacock (2000), p.428.
18 Eyre (1994), p.59.
19 Ibid., pp.60–1.
20 Ibid., p.58.
21 Peacock (2000), p.429.
22 Thompson (1999), p.107.
23 Maehler, H. (1992) 'Visitors to Elephantine: Who were they?' in Johnson, J. (ed.) *Life in a Multi-cultural society: Egypt from Cambyses to Constantine and Beyond*, Chicago, The Oriental Institute of the University of Chicago, p.211.
24 Ibid., p.211.
25 Peacock (2000), p.428 (the measurements have been converted to metres for simplicity).
26 Eyre (1994), p.64.
27 Peacock (2000), pp.426–7.
28 Thompson (2009), p.135.
29 Ibid., p.135.
30 Peacock (2000), p.428.
31 Thompson (2009), p.136.
32 Peacock (2000), p.444.
33 Grzymski, K. (1997) *Pelusium: Gateway to Egypt*, Archaeological Institute of America www.archaeology.org/online/features/pelusium/

34   Peacock (2000), p.427.
35   Thompson (2009), p.128.
36   Peacock (2000), p.426.
37   Gabra (1993), p.14.
38   Peacock (2000), p.425.
39   Sheehan (2009), p.4.
40   Jeffreys and Smith (1988), p.60.
41   Ibid., p.60.
42   Jones, M. (1997) 'Archaeological Discoveries in Doqqi and the Course of the Nile at Cairo during the Roman Period' in *MDAIK* 53, p.108.
43   Sheehan, P. (2009) 'Sailing to Babylon' in *Egyptian Archaeology* 34, p.4.
44   Peacock (2000), p.433.
45   Sheehan (2009), p.4.
46   Bagnall, R.S. (2009) *Early Christian Books in Egypt*, Oxford, Princeton University Press, p.2.
47   Thompson (2009), p.145.
48   Bagnall (2009), p.3.
49   Thompson (2009), p.154.
50   Ibid., p.142.
51   Edwards, M. (2007) 'The Beginnings of Christianization' in Lenski, N. (ed.) (2007) *Age of Constantine*, Cambridge, Cambridge University Press, p.150.
52   Peacock (2000), p.445.
53   Ibid., p.441.
54   Bagnall (2009), p.64.
55   Hillier et al (2007), p.1011.
56   Banaji (2001), p.203.
57   Thompson (2009), p.153.
58   Edwards (2007), p.144.
59   El Daly (2005), p.104.
60   Collins (2001), p.15.
61   Ibid., p.18.
62   Bagnall (2009), pp.18–9.
63   Edwards (2006), p.138.
64   Bagnall (2009), p.3.
65   Thompson (2009), p.157.
66   Pankhurst, R. (2000) 'Ethiopia's alleged control of the Nile' in Erlich, H. and Gershoni, I. (2000) *The Nile: histories, cultures, myths*, London, Lynne Rienner Publishers, p.25.
67   Bagnall (2009), p.61.
68   Thompson (2009), p.157.
69   El Daly (2005), pp.61, 44.
70   Peacock (2000), p.441.
71   Thompson (2009), p.150.
72   Gabra (1993), p.15.
73   Ibid., p.16.
74   Thompson (2009), p.143.
75   Gabra (1993), p.16.
76   Thompson (2009), p.161.
77   Collins (2001), p.20.
78   Gabra (1993), pp.16–7.

9 RIVER OF PARADISE AND RECEPTACLE OF THE RAINS OF HEAVEN

 1   Gabra (1993), pp.16–7.

2   El Daly (2005), p.20.
3   Ibn Fadl Allah in El Daly (2005), p.24.
4   Frantz-Murphy, G. (1999) 'Land Tenure in Egypt in the First Five centuries of Islamic Rule (seventh–twelfth Centuries AD)' in Bowman, A. and Rogan, E. (1999) *Agriculture in Egypt: from pharaonic to modern times*, Oxford, Oxford University Press, p.242.
5   Ibid., p.238.
6   Ibid., p.245.
7   Keenan, J.G. (1999) 'Fayyum Agriculture at the End of the Ayyubid Era: Nabulsi's Survey' in Bowman, A. and Rogan, E. (1999) *Agriculture in Egypt: from Pharaonic to modern times*, Oxford, Oxford University Press, p.290.
8   Ibid., p.295.
9   Ibid., p.294.
10 Le Quesne, C. (1995) 'Old Cairo: Fortress into City' in *Egyptian Archaeology* 7, p.4.
11 Bianquis, T. (1999) 'Autonomous Egypt from Ibn Tulun to Kafur, 868–969' in Petry, C. (ed.) *The Cambridge History of Egypt; Islamic Egypt, 640–1517*, Cambridge, Cambridge University Press, p.88.
12 Thomspson (2009), p.167.
13 Gayraud, R.P. (2001) 'Medieval Aqueducts of Fustât' in *Egyptian Archaeology* 19, p.35.
14 Ibid., p.34.
15 Thompson (2009), p.175.
16 Udovitch, A.I. (1999) 'International Trade and the Medieval Egyptian Countryside' in Bowman, A. and Rogan, E. (1999) *Agriculture in Egypt: from Pharaonic to modern times*, Oxford, Oxford University Press, p.268.
17 Ibid., p.269.
18 Northrup, L. (1998) 'The Bahri Mamluk sultanate, 1250–1390' in Petry, C. (ed.) *The Cambridge History of Egypt; Islamic Egypt, 640–1517*, Cambridge, Cambridge University Press, p.282.
19 Bianquis (1999), p.86.
20 Collins (2001), p.16.
21 Bianquis (1999), p.98.
22 Collins (2001), p.16.
23 Budge (1901), p.92.
24 Frantz-Murphy (1999), p.244.
25 Sheehan (2009), p.6.
26 El Daly (2005), p.126.
27 Hassan, F. (2007) 'Droughts, famine and the collapse of the Old Kingdom: re-reading Ipuwer' in Hawass, Z. and Richards, J. (eds) *The Archaeology and Art of ancient Egypt; essays in honor of David B. O'Connor*, Cairo, Annales du sevices des Antiquitiés de l'Egypte, Cahir, No.36, p.361.
28 Pankhurst (2000), p.26.
29 Ibid., p.28.
30 Gayraud (2001), p.6.
31 El Daly (2005), p.34.
32 Ibid., p.37.
33 Ibid., p.35.
34 Gayraud (2001), p.7.
35 Ibid., p.8.
36 El Daly (2005), p.33.
37 Jones (1997), p.106.
38 Ibid., p.107.
39 El Daly (2005), p.10.
40 Ibid., p.86.
41 Ibid., p.82.

42   Ibid., p.124.
43   Ibid., p.90.
44   Ibid., p.113.
45   Ibid., p.81.
46   Ibid., p.89.
47   Ibid., p.18.
48   Thompson (2009), p.184.
49   The medieval historian Ibn Khaldun (1332–1406 CE) describes the city in Thompson (2009), p.201.
50   Thompson (2009), p.197.

10 A DONKEY RIDE AND A BOATING TRIP INTERSPERSED WITH RUINS

1   Anderson, R. and Fawzy, I. (eds) (1987) *Egypt in 1800*, London, IMPADS Associates, p.7.
2   Neret, G. (2002) *Description De L'Egypte*, London, Taschen, p.12.
3   Tyldesley, J. (2005) *Egypt; How a lost civilisation was rediscovered*, London, BBC Books, p.44.
4   Chandler, D.G. (1994) *On the Napoleonic Wars; Collected Essays*, London, Greenhill Books, p.58.
5   Thompson (2009), p.220.
6   Anderson and Fawsy (1987), p.7.
7   Bednarski, A. (2005) *Holding Egypt; tracing the reception of the 'Description de l'Égypte' in nineteenth-century Great Britain*, London, Golden House, p.13.
8   Marcos (2000), p.35.
9   Chandler (1994), p.56.
10   Ibid., p.59.
11   Thompson (2008), p.222.
12   Chandler (1994), p.71.
13   Tyldesley (2005), p.51.
14   Ibid., p.55.
15   Cartouches were the ovals surrounding the king's birth name and coronation names. The name 'cartouche' was given by Napolean's army and is the French for 'gun cartridge' due to their shape.
16   Tyldesley (2005), p.66.
17   Reeves and Wilkinson (1996), p.64.
18   Ibid., p.54.
19   Tyldesley (2005), p.103.
20   Vittorini, S. (2004) 'Travels and Collections as metaphors of Colonial Domination' in Bresciani, E. and Betrò, M. (eds) *Egypt in India; Egyptian Antiquities in Indian Museums*, Piza, Piza University Press, p.24.
21   Tyldesley (2005), p.92.
22   Manley (1991), p.14.
23   Brendon, P. (1991) *Thomas Cook; 150 years of popular Tourism*, London, Secker & Warburg, p. 120.
24   Brendon (1991), p.120.
25   Hamilton, J. (2005) *Thomas Cook; The Holiday Maker*, Stroud, Sutton Publishing, p.167.
26   Brendon (1991), p.132.
27   Budge, E.A.W. (1906) *Cook's Handbook for Egypt and the Sudan*, London, Thomas Cook & Sons, p.2.
28   Brendon (1991), p.124.
29   Ibid., p.121.
30   Hamilton (2005), p.181.
31   Faulkner in Brendon (1991), p.200.
32   Manley (1991), p.171.
33   Brendon (1991), p.125.
34   Manley (1991), p.164.
35   Budge (1906), p.20.

36   Manley (1991), p.14.
37   Tyldesley (2005), p.44.
38   Hamilton (2005), p.180.
39   Brendon (1991), p.130.
40   Hamilton (2005), p.199.
41   Ibid., p.169.
42   Manley (1991), p.75. John Ripley in 1871 on the third trip with Cook would sit in Shepheard's watching the tourists return.
43   Brendon (1991), p.132.
44   Manley (1991), pp.74–5.
45   Budge (1906), p.43.
46   Brendon (1991), p.136.
47   Pierre Loti (1910) in Manley (1991), p.170.
48   Manley (1991), p.208.
49   Brendon (1991), p.126.
50   Vittorini (2004), p.27.
51   Budge (1906), p.20.

11 PROSPERITY AND WATER GO HAND IN HAND

1   Thompson (2008), pp.225–6.
2   Ibid., p.229.
3   Budge (1901), p.51.
4   Thompson (2008), p.228.
5   Ibid., p.229.
6   Fagan (1992), p.252.
7   Budge (1901), p.92.
8   Kerisel (1999), p.99.
9   Reeves and Wilkinson (1996), p.86.
10   Little (1965), p.186.
11   Three letters by Belzoni to Drovetti http://www.travellersinegypt.org/archives/2004/09/the_initial_difficulties_of_an.html.
12   Hassan, F. (2005) *The Infernal Water Machine; Inside an arduous hydraulic project conceived by a resourceful circus performer and incipient Egyptologist*, accessed on http://www.egypttoday.com/article.aspx?ArticleID=5888.
13   Hassan (2005).
14   Ibid.
15   Little (1965), p.11.
16   Ibid., p.234.
17   Budge (1901), p.92.
18   Ibid., pp.83–6.
19   Collins (2000), p.246.
20   Thompson (2008), pp.237–8.
21   Little (1965), p.11.
22   Thompson (2008), p.247.
23   Ibid., p.240.
24   Little (1965), p.12.
25   Ibid., p.107.
26   Ibid., p.6.
27   Collins (2000), p.251.
28   Little (1965), p.40.
29   Ibid., p.52.

30   Ibid., p.144.
31   Ibid., p.76.
32   Ibid., p.233.
33   Macquitty, W. (1976) *Island of Isis: Philae, temple of the Nile*, London, Macdonald and Jane, p.158.
34   Collins (2001), p.4.
35   Malleson, C. (2009) 'Survey in the area around Medinet el-Gurob' in *Egyptian Archaeology* 34, p.31.
36   Cross (2009), p.8.
37   Gohary, J. (1998) *Guide to the Nubian monuments on Lake Nasser*, Cairo, American University in
     Cairo Press, pp.83–6.
38   Wright, G.R.H. (1972) *Kalabsha; the preserving of the temple*, Berlin, Mann Verlag GmbH, p.16.
39   Ibid., p.21.
40   Little (1965), p.169.
41   Wright (1972), p.29.
42   Gohary (1998), p.28.
43   Wright (1972), p.37.
44   Macquitty (1976), p.156.
45   Little (1965), p.200.
46   Macquitty (1976), p.165.
47   Little (1965), p.194.
48   Ibid., pp.191–2.
49   Ibid., p.174.
50   Ibid., p.184.
51   Tyldesley (2005), p.231.
52   Little (1965), p.229.
53   Kerisel (1999), p.150.
54   Zahran, M. (2000) 'Urban design and eco-tourism; the Alexandria Comprehensive Master
     Plan' in Mostafa, M.H., Grimal, N. and Nakashima, D. (eds) (2000) *Underwater Archaeology and
     Coastal Management; Focus on Alexandria*, Paris, Unesco Publishing, pp.187–8.
55   Budge (1901), p.87.
56   Budge (1901), p.54.
57   Kerisel (1999), p.149.

EPILOGUE: WHOEVER DRINKS WATER FROM THE NILE IS SURE TO RETURN

1   El Bastawissi, I. (2000) 'Need for a coastal Management plan; the Alexandria case' in
     Mostafa, M.H., Grimal, N. and Nakashima, D. (eds) (2000) *Underwater Archaeology and Coastal
     Management; Focus on Alexandria*, Paris, Unesco Publishing, p.164.
2   Hawass (1998).
3   Hawass, Z. (2009) *Keeping the Great Sphinx's Paws Dry* from http://drhawass.com/blog/
     keeping-great-sphinx%E2%80%99s-paws-dry, p.1.
4   Johnson, R. (2001) 'Luxor's Ground water problems' in *Egyptian Archaeology* 19 (Autumn) p.10.
5   Brand, P. (2001) 'Rescue Epigraphy in the Hypostyle Hall at Karnak' in *Egyptian Archaeology*
     19 (Autumn) p.11.
6   Johnson (2001) p.10.
7   Spencer, P. (1999) 'Groundwater Issues at Karnak Temple' in *Egyptian Archaeology* 15, p.2.
8   Hawass (2009).
9   Bunbury (2009).
10   Marcos (2000), p.36.
11   El-Aref, N. (2006) 'Under the Waves' in *Al Ahram Weekly* accessed on http://weekly.ahram.
     org.eh/200/803/hr1.htm.
12   Morcos, S., Tongring, N., Halim, Y. El-Abbadi, M and Awad, H. (2003) 'Towards Integrated
     Management of Alexandria's Coastal Heritage', Coastal Region and Small Island Paper 14.

13   El Aref, (2006).

14   Morcos et el (2003).

15   Tongring, N. and Driscoll, N.W. (2000) 'Proposed survey of Alexandria Harbours by a sonar sub-bottom profiler' in Mostafa, M.H., Grimal, N. and Nakashima, D. (eds) (2000) *Underwater Archaeology and Coastal Management; Focus on Alexandria*, Paris, Unesco Publishing, p.103.

16   Goddio (2000) p.61.

17   Marcos (2000), p.36.

18   El Aref (2006).

19   Ibid.

20   Ibid.

21   Ibid.

22   Zahran (2000) p.185.

23   Morcos et al (2003).

24   Tongring and Driscoll (2000), p.103.

25   Ibid., p.104.

26   Empereur (2000), p.58.

27   Lutley and Bunbury (2008), p.4.

28   Ibid., p.5.

29   Ibid., p.3.

30   Cross (2009), p.7.

31   Partridge (1996), p.72.

INDEX